LGBTQ+ Issues in Criminology and Criminal Justice

This book presents six scholarly examinations of emerging issues in criminology and criminal justice as they impact LGBTQ+ people. It brings together contributions from leading international researchers exploring the needs of people of diverse sexual orientations and gender identities in the criminal justice context.

In addition to focusing on how sexual orientation and gender identity impact access to justice for LGBTQ+ persons, this book explores how to improve the work of justice practitioners, policing, and corrections in ways that address the unique needs of LGBTQ+ clients. Specific chapters include the following: a study of support for myths about male rape victims and how indicators of intolerance might shape such beliefs; two examinations of police responses to same-sex intimate partner violence, including an exploration of the role of mandatory arrest policies; an investigation into the barriers LGBTQ+ people face when attempting to access police liaison officers; an analysis of how media coverage framed the 2016 Pulse nightclub shooting in Orlando, Florida; and suggestions for creating safer and more effective interventions for LGBTQ+ women and girls who are correctional clients.

LGBTQ+ Issues in Criminology and Criminal Justice will be a key resource for academics, researchers, and advanced students of criminology and criminal justice, law, victimology, policing, corrections, research methods, sociology, and media studies. The chapters in this book were originally published in the journal *Criminal Justice Studies.*

Matthew Ball is a foundational scholar in queer criminology, researching at the intersections of sexuality, gender, and justice. He is the author of *Criminology and Queer Theory: Dangerous Bedfellows?* and co-editor of *Queering Criminology* and four other edited volumes in queer criminology.

Henry F. Fradella is the author or co-author of 12 books and nearly 120 articles, reviews, book chapters, and scholarly commentaries on legal issues in criminal justice. He specializes in the intersection of law with the social sciences, most frequently with emphases in either forensic psychology or human sexuality.

LGBTQ+ Issues in Criminology and Criminal Justice

Edited by
Matthew Ball and Henry F. Fradella

Routledge
Taylor & Francis Group
LONDON AND NEW YORK

First published 2024
by Routledge
4 Park Square, Milton Park, Abingdon, Oxon, OX14 4RN

and by Routledge
605 Third Avenue, New York, NY 10158

Routledge is an imprint of the Taylor & Francis Group, an informa business

British Library Cataloguing-in-Publication Data
A catalogue record for this book is available from the British Library

ISBN13: 978-1-032-59413-2 (hbk)
ISBN13: 978-1-032-59414-9 (pbk)
ISBN13: 978-1-003-45458-8 (ebk)

DOI: 10.4324/9781003454588

Typeset in Myriad Pro
by codeMantra

Publisher's Note
The publisher accepts responsibility for any inconsistencies that may have arisen during the conversion of this book from journal articles to book chapters, namely the inclusion of journal terminology.

Contents

Citation Information

The chapters in this book, except for Chapter 6, were originally published in the journal *Criminal Justice Studies*, volume 33, issue 3 (2020). Chapter 6 was originally published in volume 34, issue 1 (2021) of the same journal. When citing this material, please use the original page numbering for each article, as follows:

Preface

Preface to the special issue
Matthew Ball and Henry F. Fradella
Criminal Justice Studies, volume 33, issue 3 (2020) pp. 193–194

Chapter 1

Male rape in context: measures of intolerance and support for male rape myths (MRMs)
Christina DeJong, Skyler J. Morgan and Alison Cox
Criminal Justice Studies, volume 33, issue 3 (2020) pp. 195–212

Chapter 2

Police response to same-sex intimate partner violence in the marriage equality era
Lynn A. Addington
Criminal Justice Studies, volume 33, issue 3 (2020) pp. 213–230

Chapter 3

Domestic violence mandatory arrest policies and arrests for same-sex and opposite-sex intimate partner violence after legalization of same-sex marriage in the United States
Alesha Durfee and Leigh Goodmark
Criminal Justice Studies, volume 33, issue 3 (2020) pp. 231–255

Chapter 4

Barriers stopping LGBTI people from accessing LGBTI police liaison officers: analysing interviews with community and police
Angela Dwyer, Matthew Ball, Murray Lee, Thomas Crofts and Christine Bond
Criminal Justice Studies, volume 33, issue 3 (2020) pp. 256–275

Chapter 5

An act of terror and an act of hate: national elite and populace newspaper framing of pulse nightclub shooting
Jace L. Valcore and Kevin Buckler
Criminal Justice Studies, volume 33, issue 3 (2020) pp. 276–296

Chapter 6

What staff need to know: using elements of gender responsive programming to create safer environments for system-involved LGBTQ girls and women
Lindsay Kahle Semprevivo and Jill Leslie Rosenbaum
Criminal Justice Studies, volume 34, issue 1 (2021) pp. 1–15

Notes on Contributors

Lynn A. Addington is Professor in the Department of Justice, Law and Criminology at American University, Washington, DC, USA. Her research focuses on fatal and non-fatal violent victimization (with an emphasis on adolescents, emerging adults, and school environments) as well as policy responses for preventing violence and serving victims.

Matthew Ball is a foundational scholar in queer criminology, researching at the intersections of sexuality, gender, and justice. He is the author of *Criminology and Queer Theory: Dangerous Bedfellows?* and co-editor of *Queering Criminology* and four other edited volumes in queer criminology.

Christine Bond is Associate Professor at the School of Criminology and Criminal Justice and a member of the Griffith Criminology Institute at Griffith University, Australia. She has held positions at the University of Queensland and Queensland University of Technology, Brisbane, Australia. She also worked as a research officer for the then Criminal Justice Commission (Queensland).

Kevin Buckler is Professor of Criminal Justice at the University of Houston-Downtown, USA. His criminal justice-related interests and published works are in the areas of procedure and evidence, media coverage, and U.S. Supreme Court decision-making.

Alison Cox, PhD, is Assistant Professor in the Department of Sociology, Anthropology, and Criminology at the University of Northern Iowa, Cedar Falls, USA. Her research interests include corrections, specifically the prisoner-family relationship, barriers to visitation, and re-entry.

Thomas Crofts is Professor at the School of Law and Department of Social and Behavioural Sciences at the City University of Hong Kong, Hong Kong, and Professor (fractional) at the School of Law at Northumbria University, Newscastle upon Tyne, UK. He researches the criminal responsibility of, and for, children, comparative criminal law, and criminal law reform.

Christina DeJong, PhD, is Associate Professor Emerita in the School of Criminal Justice at Michigan State University, East Lansing, USA. Her research interests include gender, sexuality and justice, genocide and human rights, and interpersonal violence.

Alesha Durfee is Professor of and Chair of Women's and Gender Studies at Saint Louis University, USA. Her research, teaching, and service focus on legal interventions in cases of domestic violence, as well as the use of structural intersectionality, to analyze protection orders and mandatory arrest policies.

Angela Dwyer is Associate Professor of Police Studies and Emergency Management at the School of Social Sciences at the University of Tasmania, Hobart, Australia, and Deputy Director of the Tasmanian Institute of Law Enforcement Studies. Angela conducts research on the intersection between sexuality, gender diversity, and criminal justice.

Henry F. Fradella is the author or co-author of 12 books and nearly 120 articles, reviews, book chapters, and scholarly commentaries on legal issues in criminal justice. He specializes in the intersection of law with the social sciences, most frequently with emphases in either forensic psychology or human sexuality.

Leigh Goodmark is Marjorie Cook Professor of Law and Co-director of the Clinical Law Program at the University of Maryland Carey School of Law, Baltimore, USA, where she directs the Gender Violence Clinic. Professor Goodmark's scholarship focuses on intimate partner violence.

Murray Lee is Professor of Criminology and Associate Dean of Research at the University of Sydney Law School, Australia. Murray's research focuses broadly on representations and perceptions of crime and how these lead to processes of criminalization.

Skyler J. Morgan, PhD, is an assistant professor in the School of Criminology, Criminal Justice, and Emergency Management at California State University, Long Beach, USA. His research interests include corrections, gender and sexuality in the criminal justice system, and domestic terrorism.

Jill Leslie Rosenbaum is Professor Emerita at California State University, Fullerton, USA. She has published numerous articles and book chapters on the experiences of young women in the criminal justice system. In addition, her work on the value of "art behind bars" has been published in numerous venues.

Lindsay Kahle Semprevivo is Teaching Assistant Professor of Criminology in the Department of Sociology and Anthropology at West Virginia University, USA. Her research interests focus primarily on the intersections of gender, sexual orientation, and race and ethnicity in youth violence and victimization.

Jace L. Valcore, PhD, is a Senior Data Analyst with the Denver Sheriff Department. As a researcher and educator, he is committed to equity, inclusion, and social justice. He specializes in program and learning assessment, qualitative and mixed-methods research design, data collection and analysis, report writing, academic writing and editing, teaching, and public speaking. His content area of expertise include public policy, queer criminology, policing and LGBTQ issues, hate crimes, and hate crime laws.

Preface

Matthew Ball and Henry F. Fradella

This issue of *Criminal Justice Studies* is devoted to 'Emerging Issues in Criminology and Criminal Justice for LGBTQ+ People.' In this issue, we showcase both strong empirical studies that explore a number of important issues concerning how the criminal justice system interacts with people on the basis of sexual orientation and gender identity, as well as 'think pieces' about how to improve the work of justice practitioners in ways that address the unique concerns of lesbian, gay, bisexual, transgender, and queer (LGBTQ+) clients. Specifically, Christina DeJong, Skyler Morgan, and Alison Cox examine support for myths about male rape victims within the context of how various indicators of intolerance might shape such beliefs; Lynn Addington reports on police responses to same-sex intimate partner violence; Alesha Durfee and Leigh Goodmark similarly examine the same phenomena with a focus on the role of mandatory arrest policies; Angela Dwyer and colleagues investigate the barriers people face when attempting to access police liaison officers for the LGBTQ+ community[1]; Jace Valcore and Kevin Buckler scrutinize media coverage in the aftermath of the 2016 Pulse nightclub shooting in Orlando, Florida; and Lindsay Kahle and Jill Leslie Rosenbaum offer suggestions for creating safer and more effective interventions for LGBTQ+ women and girls who are correctional clients.

We want to express our sincere gratitude to all of the people who served as peer reviewers for the articles in this volume, especially since many of them reviewed manuscripts under tight time constraints. Without the thoughtful insights the following people shared, this volume would not have been possible: Nicole Asquith (Western Sydney University), Tod Burke (Radford University), Alesha Durfee (Arizona State University), Jenna Calton (George Mason University), Roddrick Colvin (San Diego State University), Lisa Dario (Florida Atlantic University), Courtenay Daum (Colorado State University), Bianca Fileborn (The University of Melbourne), Kate Fox (Arizona State University), Brian Frederick (University of Gloucestershire), Heather Hlavka (Marquette University), Matthew Jones (The Open University), Heather Littleton (East Carolina University), Douglas Meyer (University of Virginia), Barbara Owen (California State University, Fresno), Steven Owen (Radford University), Lisa Pasko (University of Denver), James Pickles (Sheffield Hallam University), Emma Russell (La Trobe University), John Shjarback (Rowan University), Danielle Slakoff (Loyola University of New Orleans), Mary Stohr (Washington State University), Jace Valcore (University of Houston Downtown), Megan Verhagan (Arizona State University), and Allyn Walker (Old Dominion University).

We thank Dr. Richard Tewksbury, the Editor-in-Chief of *Criminal Justice Studies*, who graciously offered us the opportunity to publish some of the fantastic submissions we received in response to a call for papers in a special issue of another journal – the sheer number of which could not be accommodated in a single issue.

Finally, although there is clearly more research relevant to sexual orientation and gender identity that needs to be addressed beyond what the six articles in this volume can do, we believe this issue of the *Criminal Justice Studies* is a step in the right direction. But special issues of journals ought not be the routine way in which these critical lines of scholarly inquiry are presented. Criminology and criminal justice lag behind other social sciences and the humanities in incorporating sexual orientation and gender identity into research. We call on our colleagues to include sexual orientation and gender identity in their research. And we call on peer reviewers and journal editors to insist that these vitally important dimensions of people's identities are not ignored in mainstream criminological scholarship.

Note

1. Dr. Ball played no role in the consideration of whether this manuscript would be accepted for publication. Dr. Fradella made that decision after receiving blind reviews that recommended that the paper be published.

Male rape in context: measures of intolerance and support for male rape myths (MRMs)

Christina DeJong, Skyler J. Morgan and Alison Cox

ABSTRACT

Research on myths about male rape victims and offenders indicates that men and heterosexual individuals tend to believe myths about male rape (MRMs), as do individuals with negative attitudes toward gay men. Many who support male rape myths assume that both male victims of rape and offenders are usually gay, or that straight men cannot be raped. Studies on MRM have portrayed male rape in an 'everyday life' context, but myths about male rape are likely shaped by its portrayal in film, television and popular culture. For example, respondents may attribute more blame to victims who are incarcerated as opposed to a victim raped by a stranger near their home. In this study, we assess support for myths about male rape victims and whether the context of the situation and various indicators of intolerance play a role in their beliefs. Specifically, we present four fictional scenarios of male rape to respondents: prison, in the military, during a conflict situation, and on a college campus. We find that respondents are less likely to support MRMs in the context of the military, and that race and gender also explain support for MRMs. Measures of intolerance are positively related to support for MRMs, with sexism having the strongest relationship with support.

Introduction

Female rape myths have been studied extensively since Burt's (1980) groundbreaking work on the subject, but considerably less attention has been paid to myths about male rape. Measures created by Struckman-Johnson and Struckman-Johnson (1992) to assess support for male rape myths (MRMs) have been used frequently in the extant literature to understand the factors that influence and shape acceptance of MRMs (Chapleau, Oswald, & Russell, 2008; Davies, Gilston, & Rogers, 2012; Kassing, Beesley, & Frey, 2005; Turhcik & Edwards, 2012), but there are still gaps in our knowledge in this area. The lack of research on MRMs could be due to the relative invisibility of male rape as a social phenomenon. Men are less likely to report rape victimization than women (Pino & Meier, 1999). Men also face different barriers to reporting than women, including homophobia, stigma, and a general lack of education and acknowledgment of the issue (Scarce, 1997).

Male rape is also highly stereotyped in popular culture, and MRMs may depend upon the context in which these events occur (Turhcik & Edwards, 2012). For example, there are strong stereotypes about male rape and sexual assault in prison, and these may affect how individuals perceive rape in prison as compared to rape in other contexts. Increased awareness of male rape in other contexts, such as conflict areas or in the military, can also shape perceptions of male rape and may perpetuate myths specific to those contexts. Studies of support for MRMs, however, have not investigated whether the context of male rape can help explain variation in support, or how measures of intolerance may be dependent on context.

The goal of this article is to determine whether the context of a male rape influences the acceptance of MRMs. In this paper, we use existing measures of MRMs and intolerance to determine whether support for MRMs depends on the circumstances of the assault. Specifically, we assess support for MRMs in four different contexts: a college campus, a prison, a military facility, and a conflict zone. In addition, we analyze the importance of other variables that have been demonstrated to have an impact on support for MRMs, including respondent characteristics (gender, race, religion, sexuality) and measures of intolerance. College students at a large public university were surveyed to determine the degree to which they support myths about MRMs, and whether the context of the situation and indicators of intolerance play a role in those beliefs.

Measuring male rape myths (MRMs)

Struckman-Johnson and Struckman-Johnson (1992) conducted one of the first studies of MRMs and identified three common themes comprising support for such myths: denial myths, blame myths, and trauma myths. In addition to these three themes, there is a common myth surrounding male rape that both victims and offenders must be gay (Tomlinson & Harrison, 1998). All four of these myths are discussed below.

Denial myths – 'male rape can't happen'

One of the male rape myths identified by Struckman-Johnson and Struckman-Johnson (1992) is the myth that men cannot be raped. This myth is rooted in the assumption that men are in control of their sexual activity and, therefore, cannot be a target of assault (Groth & Burgess, 1980). In their original work, Struckman-Johnson and Struckman-Johnson (1992) examined college students' beliefs in this myth with two items, including 'It is impossible for a man (or woman) to rape a man' and 'Even a big, strong man can be raped by another man (or woman).' Their results indicated that men are more likely to support this MRM compared to women, and recent studies using the same scale replicated these findings (Chapleau et al., 2008; Rosenstein & Carroll, 2015). Although there are gender differences found in the support for this MRM, Struckman-Johnson and Struckman-Johnson (1992) reported an overall lack of strong evidence for support of this myth and connected their findings to 'the prevailing social climate of receptivity and understanding for female rape victims' (p. 96). In addition, Chapleau et al. (2008) found that of the three types of MRMs (denial, blame, trauma), denial myths were the least supported overall.

Blame myths – 'male rape victims are to blame for their rape'

Similar to victim-blaming in female rape, the blame myths for male rape place culpability and responsibility on the male victim, because they should have more agency in the situation. The survey created by Struckman-Johnson and Struckman-Johnson (1992) measured this MRM with two items, including 'Most men who are raped by a man (or woman) are somewhat to blame for not being more careful' and 'Most men who are raped by a man (or woman) are somewhat to blame for not escaping or fighting off the man.' These items place blame on the victim in the rape as opposed to the perpetrator. Similar to denial myths, men are more likely to support the two items that embodied the blame myths when compared to women (Struckman-Johnson & Struckman-Johnson, 1992). In addition, there are higher levels of support of blame myths for both men and women participants when the perpetrator of the rape is a female instead of male, which indicates that people are more likely to blame male rape victims when the perpetrator is female. Furthermore, there tends to be more support for of blame myths compared to the other two categories of MRM – denial and trauma (Chapleau et al., 2008). Similar to denial myths, men are more likely to support blame myths as compared to women (Chapleau et al., 2008; Rosenstein & Carroll, 2015).

Trauma myths – 'getting raped doesn't really upset men'

MRMs surrounding trauma minimize the psychological trauma of male rape victims and are rooted in the misconception that traditional masculinity does not contain emotionality (Struckman-Johnson & Struckman-Johnson, 1992). Struckman-Johnson and Struckman-Johnson (1992) reported that the trauma MRMs were the least supported among participants compared to the other types of MRMs; however, Chapleau et al. (2008) found the blame subscale to have the second most supported MRMs among participants between blame (highest) and denial (lowest). Consistent with the other common MRMs themes, trauma myths in which the rape victim is a male were more likely to be supported by male respondents than female respondents (Chapleau et al., 2008; Rosenstein & Carroll, 2015; Struckman-Johnson & Struckman-Johnson, 1992).

Sexuality myths – 'men who are raped (or who rape other men) must be gay'

In addition to the three myths identified by Struckman-Johnson and Struckman-Johnson (1992), some hold the belief that both victims and offenders of male rape must be gay (Tomlinson & Harrison, 1998). This is based on the stereotype that 'real men' cannot be raped and, therefore, rape can only happen to gay men who are already culturally emasculated (Lisak, 1993). Turhcik and Edwards (2012) explain the focus on victim sexuality as one rooted in traditional aspects of masculinity and femininity. Due to socially constructed beliefs about the characteristics of 'real men' in heteronormative cultures (*i.e.* those who are not submissive, emotional, or compliant), men who are raped must not be 'real men,' and therefore must be gay.

In addition, there are strong cultural beliefs that only gay men rape other men (Anderson, 2007; Donnelly & Kenyon, 1996), which may stem from the common misunderstanding that rape is about sex rather than power. However, men who commit rape against other men are typically not motivated by a desire for sex, but for control, revenge, or sadism/degradation (Groth & Burgess, 1980). Because of this, men who would otherwise identify as 'straight' can be motivated to commit rape against a male victim. The ways in which these rape myths are influenced will be discussed in the next section.

Factors explaining support for male rape myths

Individual characteristics – gender & sexuality

Consistent with the literature on female rape myths, gender is a significant predictor of support for MRMs, with male respondents more supportive of MRMs than female respondents (Chapleau et al., 2008; Davies et al., 2012; Rosenstein & Carroll, 2015; Struckman-Johnson & Struckman-Johnson, 1992). Although there are gender differences found for both female and male rape myth acceptance, there is some disagreement on the underlying reason for men being more likely to accept rape myths. Research on female rape myths has often linked the gender disparities in rape myth support to anti-women attitudes, greater tolerance of sexual aggression, and traditional gender roles assigned to women (Feild, 1978; Jenkins & Dambrot, 1987; Lonsway & Fitzgerald, 1995). In contrast, studies finding that men are more likely to support both male and female rape myths indicate that anti-women attitudes are not necessarily the cause of their female rape myth support. Rather, they speculate that men are generally more likely to support rape myths and maybe less emotionally connected to issues surrounding rape (Chapleau et al., 2008; Davies, Pollard, & Archer, 2001; Struckman-Johnson & Struckman-Johnson, 1992).

Few studies have examined the impact of respondent sexuality on support for MRMs, with only one finding a relationship in the expected direction – that lesbian, gay, bisexual, transgender, or queer (LGBTQ) respondents are less likely to support rape myths – although this finding disappeared after controlling for attitudinal factors related to gender and sexuality norms (Walfield, 2018). But gender and sexuality may *interact* to help explain support for MRMs. Although men are generally found to be most supportive of male rape myths, there are significant differences when sexuality is introduced as a factor. Davies and McCartney (2003) found an intersection between gender and sexuality, with straight men having the most supportive attitudes toward MRMs, and gay men being the most opposed to MRMs; however, they did not control for any other factors. This research has provided some insight into how sexuality may predict support for male rape myths, but unfortunately most research on MRMs has not included the sexuality of the respondent as a variable (Chapleau et al., 2008; Rosenstein & Carroll, 2015; Struckman-Johnson & Struckman-Johnson, 1992).

Measures of intolerance – homophobia, sexism, & racism

The most common indicator of support for MRMs is homophobia, which can be used as a victim-blaming mechanism (Burt & DeMello, 2002; Ford, Liwag-McLamb, & Foley, 1998; Kassing et al., 2005). Homophobia is one aspect of heteronormative culture that shapes individual attitudes, including perceptions of male rape. As indicated by Sivakumaran (2007), 'Society considers any [sexual contact between two men] to be indicative of homosexuality, regardless of any element of coercion. Given the prevalence of homophobia in society, this amounts to a "taint" on the part of the victim of the rape' (p. 1274). One study determined that homophobia was not related to support for rape myths after controlling for other variables (Davies et al., 2012), a finding that contradicted Kassing et al. (2005) original analysis. Unfortunately, collinearity between the independent variables may have masked the effect of homophobia on MRMs in the study by Davies et al. (2012), and it seems vital to analyze measures of intolerance separately to disentangle which may be most relevant for explaining support for MRMs.

To date, only two studies have examined the connection between sexism and MRMs (Chapleau et al., 2008; Davies et al., 2012). Chapleau et al. (2008) determined that both benevolent sexism and hostile sexism can be related to MRMs. Benevolent sexism is an attitude that praises women or men for being traditionally feminine or masculine, while hostile sexism slanders women and men who reject traditional gender roles. Davies et al. (2012) extended their work and found a moderate and positive association between support for MRMs and hostile sexism at the bivariate level. While we have an idea of how sexism functions in the context of MRM acceptance, more research is necessary to understand the connection.

Although racism is a measure of intolerance that has been studied within the context of female rape myths (Aosved & Long, 2006; Suarez & Gadalla, 2010), to the best of our knowledge, no studies have analyzed the association between MRMs support and racism. This is not surprising considering the vast disparities in attention given to female rape myths compared to MRMs. To better understand MRM support, racism should be also considered as a measure of intolerance and examined with regard to support for MRMs.

The context of male rape and associated stereotypes

Context is vitally important when studying attitudes and myths about rape (Check & Malamuth, 1983; Turhcik & Edwards, 2012). Most studies of MRMs have focused on date rape and stranger rape scenarios; that is, rape myths are assessed in the context of 'normal life.' There has been little examination, however, of support for rape myths in different contexts. Because MRMs are based on stereotypes, we posit that investigating the context of male rape is necessary in order to explain MRMs. Specifically, we use scenario research to investigate male rape in prison, the military, during conflict situations, and compare support for MRMs to male rape in 'normal' situations – in this case, a college campus in the United States.

Prison

Perhaps the most common stereotypes about male rape are generated from the prison context (Eigenberg & Baro, 2003; Mason, 2006; Turhcik & Edwards, 2012). Much of the public's perception of male rape in prison is shaped by narratives created by the media. Turhcik and Edwards (2012) argue that the media tends to depict male rape in prison as either serious or humorous, and that male rape in prison is a legitimate consequence for men who break the law. These perspectives indicate the depiction of prison rape in the media can be both representative and misleading of the reality of male rape. For example, while we know male rape in prisons is not a common occurrence, research has indicated that the media pushes a narrative that incidents are common and inevitable (Eigenberg &

Baro, 2003). We, therefore, expect that respondents will attribute higher levels of blame to rape victims in prison, given that they are incarcerated for committing crime.

Conflict

Sexual violence is a common occurrence in war and conflict situations (Chynoweth, 2017), yet the rape of men in conflict has received little attention in the media. In fact, it is unclear how knowledgeable the public is about rape during conflict in general, regardless of the victim's gender. The wars in the Democratic Republic of the Congo and Syria have documented the rape of men and have received some media attention, but these stories are still few and far between (for example, 'We need to talk about male rape': DR Congo survivor speaks out, 2017). In addition, most reports are not published in mainstream news outlets and are more commonly published by human rights organizations, such as Amnesty International, The World Health Organization, and the International Center for Transitional Justice (Amnesty International, 2012; Kapur & Muddell, 2016; Krug, Dahlberg, Mercy, Zwi, & Lozano, 2002).

There is little research on the extent of public awareness of male rape in conflict. Perhaps the most publicized occurrence of male sexual assault is the sexual torture of inmates at Abu Ghraib prison in Iraq. A significant number of studies have investigated both the media framing of this event as well as public perceptions. In the United States specifically, media reports avoided the word 'torture' and instead preferred words such as 'abuse' or 'mistreatment' (Jones & Sheets, 2009). The framing of the case in this way serves to minimize sexual victimization in the eyes of the public; indeed, at least one popular conservative radio host described the sexual torture of male detainees as akin to a fraternity initiation, with American soldiers 'blowing off steam during a stressful situation' (Meyer, 2004, para. 6).

It is unclear as to what degree respondents will support MRMs when confronted with a male rape in conflict context. The minimization of the impact of sexual violence is consistent with the myth that 'male rape is not serious,' and therefore we suspect that the conflict scenario may have higher levels of support for that aspect of MRMs.

Military

The hyper-masculine culture of most military organizations has contributed to high rates of sexual assault and rape in their ranks (O'Brien, Keith, & Shoemaker, 2015; Turchik et al., 2013; Turhcik & Edwards, 2012). Male victims of rape in the military may fear reporting their victimization, lest they be labeled as 'gay' or feminized by their comrades (Nelson, 2002). In addition, high levels of homophobia in the military have led to anti-gay violence against male soldiers, which can take the form of physical violence and sexual assault.[1]

There has been much public attention to the issue of sexuality in the armed forces. Policies regarding service by members of the LGBTQ community have shifted since the early 1980s, when LGBTQ citizens were banned from serving in the armed forces, frequently labeled as being mentally ill (Herek, 1993). This changed under the Clinton Presidency, who shifted the policy to 'Don't Ask, Don't Tell,' (United States Department of Defense, 1993), with the Obama administration later removing this policy and allowing LGBTQ soldiers to serve openly (Bumiller, 2011).

The Trump administration, however, has banned transgender individuals from service – a decision supported by the U.S. Supreme Court ("United States Supreme Court allows Trump military transgender ban, 2019). It is unclear how these changes have impacted the perception of male rape victims in the military. Given the media focus on sexuality, the public might be more likely to perceive that male rape victims are gay, or that offenders are likely to be gay given the more open recruitment policies (even without evidence of such). On the other hand, we may see less blame of victims in the military context, as soldiers are frequently viewed as 'heroes' who 'served their country.' Therefore, we expect the military context may score lower on the 'blame' myth but higher on the items that assume the victim and/or offenders are gay.

'Normal life'

Prior studies of male rape myths discussed above use scenarios placed in the context of 'normal life' in the United Kingdom and the United States. In these scenarios, the sexual assaults occur in either public (parks, parking lots) or private spaces (apartments). The primary goal of these studies was to compare blame attributions by varying victim/offender gender and sexuality, as well as the relationship between victim and offender.

The current study

In this study, we attempt to fill the gap in our understanding of how MRMs might vary depending on the context of male rape. Specifically, our interests focus on the four main types of MRMs (denial, blame, trauma, and sexuality) to determine whether the context of male rape has an effect on support for myths (prison, conflict, military, and college). In addition, we test whether known indicators of support for MRMs are dependent on the context of the assault. Our specific research questions are:

RQ1: Does support for MRMs depend on the context of the rape, whether occurring on a college campus, in a prison, in the military, or in conflict?

RQ2: Do measures of intolerance have different impacts on support for MRMs depending on the context of the assault?

Data and methods

Data for this study were collected using a survey of undergraduate students enrolled in introductory classes at a large midwestern university. To determine whether context of the assault has an effect on support for MRMs, we presented respondents with a fictional sexual assault in four different contexts: 'normal life' (college), prison, military, and during conflict. We developed a vignette for each context based on those developed by Davies et al. (2001), changing the scene to occur either on a college campus, inside a prison, on a military base, or during a conflict (vignettes are included in the Appendix A). Respondents randomly received one of the four scenarios in their survey, along with measures of support for MRMs, measures of intolerance, and demographic information.

We used several steps in our survey design to minimize trauma to victims responding to the survey. First, upon administration of the survey, the researchers explained that the survey focused on attitudes toward sexual assault. According to our university IRB, completion of the survey was optional, and respondents could discontinue taking the survey at any time. Respondents were instructed to turn the survey face down if they chose not to participate, when they decided to stop participating (which they could do anytime), or when they completed the survey. The survey was clearly titled, 'Attitudes on Sexual Assault Survey 2018' to ensure respondents were aware of the topic.

The survey began with general questions about sexual assault to set the tone and prepare respondents for content about sexual assault. Next, we presented one (of four) random male rape scenarios to the respondents and asked questions focused on male rape myths. This section was followed by items from Intolerant Schema (Aosved, Long, & Voller, 2009), which were intended to measure homophobia, religious intolerance, racial intolerance, sexism, and classism. We ended the survey with questions on demographic characteristics. Descriptive statistics on the independent variables in the sample are contained in Table 1. A total of 318 surveys were returned, with two cases removed for failing validation,[2] and two removed because respondents were below the age of 18. Respondents in this study were mostly female, White, and in their first year of college. Most of the sample identified as heterosexual and Christian. Approximately 12% of the sample reported that they had experienced a sexual assault, and more than 60% reported they knew someone who had been sexually assaulted.

Results

The dependent variable in this study is 'support for Male Rape Myths (MRMs),' which consists of four different aspects of support. Three components of support for MRMs were predominately taken from Struckman-Johnson and Struckman-Johnson (1992), and two items were added indicating whether the respondent believes rape victims and the belief that offenders are likely (or must be) gay (Tomlinson & Harrison, 1998). The descriptive statistics on these items are presented in Table 2, with higher values indicating stronger agreement with each item. We are have arranged these by sub-scale, but Cronbach's alpha was calculated based on all items combined.

Table 2 also contains Cronbach's alpha and descriptive statistics on the intolerance items, which were grouped into scales measuring homophobia, religious intolerance, racial intolerance, sexism, and classism. Pre-testing of the survey indicated that several items from Aosved et al. (2009) intolerance scale used outdated language and were confusing to respondents. These items were reworded using more modern language, but patterns of missing data indicate other items might also have been unclear or confusing.[3] All scales were created by adding all items and dividing by the number of items to force the scale to range from 1 to 5, with lower values indicating less support for rape myths. Scale reliability ranged from .76 to .91, with the lowest scores on the sexism and homophobia scales (indicating less tolerance for sexist and homophobic beliefs), and the highest scores on the classism scale (indicating slightly more tolerance of classist beliefs).

In Table 3, we examine which independent variables are related to support for rape myths (with higher values indicating greater support for MRMs). We dropped missing data

Table 1. Descriptive Statistics on the Sample (N = 314).

	N	Valid Percent		N	Valid Percent		N	Valid Percent
Gender of respondents			Current Age			Sexuality		
Male	114	(36.3%)	18	200	(63.7%)	Heterosexual	256	(81.5%)
Female	179	(57.0%)	19	53	(16.9%)	Gay/lesbian	5	(1.6%)
Missing	21	(6.7%)	20	23	(7.3%)	Bisexual	19	(6.1%)
			21	8	(2.6%)	Queer	2	(0.6%)
			22	5	(1.6%)	Asexual	1	(0.3%)
Religion			23	3	(1.0%)	Don't know	5	(1.6%)
Christian	175	(55.7%)	*Missing*	22	(7.0%)	*Missing*	26	(8.3%)
Jewish	5	(1.6%)						
Muslim	6	(1.9%)				**Race**		
Hindu	2	(0.6%)	**Year**			White	206	(65.6%)
Buddhist	4	(1.3%)	Freshman	231	(73.1%)	Black	21	(6.7%)
Other	90	(28.7%)	Sophomore	32	(10.1%)	Latino	14	(4.5%)
Missing	32	(10.2%)	Junior	19	(6.0%)	Asian	24	(7.6%)
			Senior	12	(3.8%)	Native Am	0	(0.0%)
			Missing	22	(7.0%)	Other	24	(7.6%)
Context						*Missing*	25	(8.0%)
College	80	(25.5%)						
Prison	78	(24.8%)	**Has experienced a sexual assault**			**Knows a sexual assault victim**		
Military	79	(25.2%)	Yes	38	(12.1%)	Yes	199	(63.4%)
War/Conflict	77	(24.5%)	No	246	(78.3%)	No	89	(28.3%)
			Missing	30	(9.6%)	*Missing*	26	(8.3%)

Table 2. Support for Male Rape Myths and Intolerance Scales (N = 314)[a.]

Male Rape Myth Scale (*alpha* =.*82*)			
Subscale: Denial that male rape can happen		Mean (std dev)	Missing
It is impossible for a man to rape another man		1.95 (1.54)	7
Most charges of male rape are unfounded		3.20 (1.26)	76
Subscale: Victim-blaming			
Steve could have fought the man off		2.71 (1.12)	31
Steve could have prevented the attack		2.30 (1.11)	17
A man can prevent his own rape		2.07 (1.04)	16
Steve was to blame for walking alone at night		1.42 (.70)	5
Steve was partially responsible for the attack		1.45 (.74)	8
*Subscale: Recognition of Trauma**			
I have a lot of sympathy for Steve		4.30 (.78)	6
The police should take Steve's attack seriously		4.69 (.59)	4
The hospital should take Steve's attack seriously		4.68 (.57)	4
Steve will probably be traumatized		4.62 (.51)	8
The attacker should be charged with rape		4.78 (.51)	5
The attacker should be punished with incarceration		4.64 (.64)	18
Steve's life will be adversely affected by the attack		4.48 (.63)	18
If I were Steve, I would be very upset		4.77 (.47)	4
Gay Stereotyping			
A man who rapes another must be gay		2.24 (1.10)	10
Men who are raped by other men are more likely gay		2.09 (1.11)	45
	Cronbach's Alpha	Mean (Std Dev)	Missing
Male Rape Myths	.82	1.77 (.48)	133
Homophobia	.91	1.58 (.62)	68
Religious Intolerance[b]	.76	1.82 (.59)	155
Racial Intolerance[c]	.86	1.63 (.58)	131
Sexism	.88	1.56 (.59)	72
Classism	.87	2.36 (.81)	140

[a]All scales range from 1 (Strongly Disagree) to 5 (Strongly Agree).
[b]Only includes items that were intolerant of non-Christians. The two anti-Christian measures did not load on this scale.
[c]One item did not load on the Racial Intolerance measure and was dropped.
*Reverse coded.

for this analysis, but imputed missing values for the regression analysis. Most respondents did not voice support for male rape myths – all mean values fell between 'strongly disagree' (1) and 'disagree' (2) for each group. There were several significant differences to report; specifically, men are more likely to support male rape myths than women, which is consistent with findings from other studies. Age was significantly related to belief in male rape myths, with the 20-year old respondents reporting higher beliefs in male rape myths that the other groups according to the value of Tukey's HSD test. In terms of race, white respondents reported higher support for rape myths than nonwhite respondents. Having experienced a sexual assault and knowing the victim of a sexual assault reduces support for male rape myths. Finally, there were no significant differences in support for MRMs depending on the context of the vignette. All measures of intolerance were significantly related to the overall 'Support for MRM' Scale, with sexism having the strongest correlation.

Our regression of support for MRMs on the independent variables is contained in Table 4. Given the continuous nature of the dependent variable, we used ordinary least squares regression for this analysis. Multiple imputation using chained equations was used to

Table 3. Bivariate Associations with Male Rape Myths (N=314).[1]

Gender		Age	
Male	2.03**	18	1.74*
Female	1.59	19	1.67
		20	2.09
Sexuality (*collapsed*)		21-23	1.66
Heterosexual	1.76		
Other	1.71	Year	
		Freshman	1.76
Hometown		Sophomore	1.63
Urban	1.94	Junior	1.85
Suburban	1.70	Senior	1.70
Rural	1.75		
Multiple	1.32		
		Race (*collapsed*)	
Context		White	1.92*
College	1.87	Nonwhite	1.70
Prison	1.72		
Military	1.77	Class Type	
War/Conflict	1.73	Criminal Justice	1.77
		General Education	1.78
Respondent was victim of SA		Respondent knows a victim of SA	
Yes	1.70*	Yes	1.64**
No	1.92	No	1.93
	Scales (correlations with MRMs)		
	Homophobia	.66**	
	Religious Intolerance	.66**	
	Racial Intolerance	.65**	
	Sexism	.74**	
	Classism	.60**	

* p<.05; ** p<.01
[1]Higher values indicate greater support for Male Rape Myths.

Table 4. Multiple Regression of Male Rape Myths on Independent Variables (N=314).

Variable	Model I		Model II		Model III		Model IV		Model V		Model VI	
	Slope	(Std Err)	Slope	(Std Err)	Slope	(Std Err)	Slope	(Std Err)	Slope	(Std Err)	Slope	(Std Err)
Constant	.74	(.55)	1.43	(.54)**	1.01	(.58)	1.18	(.58)*	1.23	(.53)*	1.19	(.58)*
Female	-.05	(.06)	-.16	(.06)**	-.17	(.06)**	-.24	(.05)**	-.09	(.06)	-.18	(.06)**
Heterosexual	-.11	(.08)	-.08	(.08)	-.10	(.09)	-.12	(.08)	-.07	(.08)	-.07	(.09)
Age	.02	(.03)	.01	(.03)	.02	(.03)	.02	(.03)	.01	(.03)	.02	(.03)
Nonwhite	-.20	(.06)**	-.21	(.07)**	-.18	(.07)**	-.21	(.06)**	-.19	(.06)**	-.29	(.07)**
Christian	.01	(.05)	-.04	(.06)	.01	(.06)	.03	(.05)	.02	(.05)	.05	(.06)*
Knows Victim	-.09	(.05)	-.11	(.06)	-.11	(.06)	-.09	(.06)	-.10	(.06)	-.15	(.06)
Was Victim	-.08	(.07)	-.05	(.08)	-.05	(.08)	-.07	(.08)	-.07	(.08)	-.02	(.08)
Class Type	-.04	(.05)	-.03	(.06)	-.02	(.06)	-.07	(.05)	-.06	(.05)	-.02	(.06)
Rape Context												
Prison	.01	(.06)	.01	(.07)	-.02	(.07)	.04	(.07)	.01	(.07)	.01	(.08)
Military	-.13	(.07)*	-.08	(.07)	-.18	(.07)*	-.04	(.07)	-.06	(.07)	-.10	(.07)
war	-.07	(.07)	-.08	(.08)	-.08	(.08)	.01	(.08)	-.04	(.07)	-.05	(.08)
Homophobia	.08	(.06)	.40	(.05)**								
Religious Intol	.22	(.06)**			.45	(.05)**						
Racial Intol	-.04	(.10)					.45	(.05)**				
Sexism	.27	(.10)**							.49	(.05)**		
Classism	.08	(.05)									.31	(.04)**
R-squared	.65		.50		.52		.53		.57		.48	

*p<.05; **p<.01.

impute missing values, and due to the extent of missing cases, we imputed 40 total datasets (Graham, Olchowski, & Gilreath, 2007).

Model I contains all variables, including demographic variables and measures of intolerance. Not surprisingly, including all measures of intolerance simultaneously created problems with collinearity – we therefore present it as a baseline model to determine the impact of the demographic variables and rape context variables on support for MRMs, but note that collinearity will affect the coefficients for the intolerance measures. In Model I, the variables that significantly impact support for MRMs are race (nonwhite respondents showed less support) and military context – respondents who received the military scenario were less likely to support MRMs in that situation than for the college context (the reference category). To avoid multicollinearity and attempt to determine which of the intolerance measures are most strongly related to support for MRMs, we include one measure of intolerance in each of Models II through VI.

Respondent race is the only variable consistently related to support for MRMs across measures of intolerance – nonwhite respondents report less support for MRMs regardless of the measure of intolerance included. Gender is sometimes related to support dependent upon the measure of intolerance included, and always in the expected direction (with females less supportive of support for MRMs). All measures of intolerance were positively and significantly related to support for MRMs after controlling for context and demographic indicators.

Respondents receiving the military context reported less support for MRMs than the college context when controlling for religious intolerance, but this relationship did not exist for any other models. Finally, we ran models including interaction terms to determine whether context interacted with measures of intolerance. We found that intolerance did not have a differential effect on support for MRMs dependent on context. These models are not presented but are available upon request.

Summary and conclusions

In sum, we find that only the military context has an effect on support for MRMs, with respondents demonstrating less support for MRMs in this context. Race is consistently related to support for MRMs, with nonwhite respondents less supportive than white respondents. Depending on the model, gender is sometimes related to support for MRMs, with female respondents less likely to support. Intolerance measures were all positively related to support for MRMs, which is consistent with previous scholarship.

Of all the contexts considered in this study, we predicted that there would have been higher levels of support for victims who experience rape in prison, given the social discourse that sexual assault is part of being in prison or is seen as justifiable punishment for offenders (Man & Cronan, 2001; Singer, 2013). We did not find any difference in support for MRMs between the prison context and 'normal life,' but the context or environment of prison is a particular area of male rape that needs close attention, especially as major gaps in research remain in terms of understanding barriers and facilitators to reporting sexual assault in prisons (Kubiak, Brenner, Bybee, Campbell, & Fedock, 2018). Furthermore, given a strong relationship between homophobia and MRMs, Turhcik and Edwards (2012) remind us that these myths are based on narrow definitions of sexuality and masculinity and usually give cause to keep male victims silent. This relates directly to incarcerated victims facing barriers to reporting, as Kupers (2005) found support that the concept of toxic or hypermasculinity may thwart reporting even further in prison when compared to community settings.

Although previous studies have supported the notion that individuals often simultaneously endorse both male and female rape myths (Reitz-Krueger, Mummert, & Troupe, 2017), there is a crucial need to identify the lesser known factors supporting MRMs and victim blaming. Although sexual assault prevention programs address issues related to gender, they often focus on women as victims and therefore may fail to recognize how harmful sex-role stereotyping can be for males as well (Weisz & Black, 2009). This is particularly true for men who hold homophobic, sexist, or other beliefs that may reduce their likelihood of reporting if they are sexually victimized (Fisher & Pina, 2013; Pino & Meier, 1999; Sable, Danis, Mauzy, & Gallagher, 2006).

Tackling homophobic and sexist attitudes also plays a role in further identifying factors that lend support for MRMs. With previous studies demonstrating contradictory findings (Davies et al., 2012; Kassing et al., 2005) results point to the need to further explore homophobia and its relation to support for MRMs. Furthermore, as the sample of this study was majority heterosexual (81.5%), it is crucial that samples increase diversity of respondents, particularly being inclusive of members of the LBGTQ community.

Consistent with previous findings (Chapleau et al., 2008; Davies et al., 2012), this study indicates general sexism is a strong measure of intolerance related to support for MRMs. As others have indicated, future work in this area should investigate the impact of benevolent and hostile sexism separately (Chapleau et al., 2008).

Our findings are also consistent with previous research in that male respondents are more likely to support MRMs when compared to female respondents (Chapleau et al., 2008; Davies et al., 2012; Reitz-Krueger et al., 2017; Rosenstein & Carroll, 2015; Struckman-Johnson & Struckman-Johnson, 1992). Due to these findings, sexual assault education and prevention programs designed to disprove common myths should be geared toward men. Additionally, there is dire need for adequate and comprehensive public education on the realities of male rape and facilitation of dialogue surrounding sex-role stereotyping, homophobia, sexist attitudes, and hypermasculinity. We hope that through increased awareness, education, and preventative efforts, the general public will come to reject MRMs, which will lead to an overall understanding of male rape and encourage men and those who have experience male rape to come forward and report their victimization without shame, fear, or embarrassment.

Limitations

Our study utilized a sample of college students; thus, our findings may have low external validity and require additional testing with larger and more diverse samples. In addition, testing the instrument on college-aged students restricted the variation in respondent age; if prior studies have indicated that older respondents are more likely to support MRMs, this should be tested in the general population with a wider age range. It is especially important to increase the representation of LGBTQ respondents, to determine how sexuality may affect support for MRMs.

We also found that the Aosved et al. (2009) scales proved to be outdated for younger respondents. While most items were determined to be reliable, several items were dropped due to respondent confusion over meaning – thus, they likely were low on validity. We plan to re-test this instrument in the future using different indicators of intolerance. In addition, given that current discourse in the United States seems very driven by political affiliation, we recommend that future studies in this area include this as a covariate.

Directions for future research

Based on our findings and limitations of the study, several avenues for future research are recommended. Although it may be worthwhile to investigate differences of MRMs support among students at different types of universities (*i.e.*, large public universities, regional comprehensive universities, small liberal arts colleges, and private religious colleges), the survey instrument should be distributed among non-college samples. While rape and other forms of sexual assault tend to occur at increased rates on college campuses, responses from the general public are needed. This may assist in strengthening the reliability and validity of measures.

We recommend that researchers continue to focus on measures of intolerance, especially sexism and homophobia. While all measures of intolerance were significantly related to the overall 'Support for MRM' scale, sexism had the strongest correlation with support. Furthermore, future studies should consider refining the conceptualization of intolerance measures, particularly when studying younger populations.

Related to homophobia, there should also be a greater focus on the sexuality of respondents and whether it influences their support for male rape myths. With a majority of the sample identifying as heterosexual, future research needs stronger inclusion (and thus, representation) of those who identify as lesbian, gay, bisexual, pansexual, or queer. Gender of respondents should also be explored outside the binary to include those who identify as gender non-conforming or transgender. As gender relates to sexism, including non-binary measures of gender may produce different – or possibly more telling – results related to support for MRMs.

Finally, additional studies examining MRMs should include measures for political party given the current polarized climate in the United States, particularly with regard to gender and sexuality. Sexual assault has been a major topic of conversation in the United States after high profile cases at universities (against both female and male victims), accusations of assault against public figures, and continued discrimination against LGBTQ individuals. Given that many of these issues seem to divide the populace politically, we strongly recommend that political party affiliation be included in future research.

Notes

1. Perhaps the most serious and notable account of this is the murder of Private Barry Winchell, a soldier in the United States Army who was murdered by a fellow soldier. According to court testimony, Winchell had endured months of harassment about his sexuality, eventually resulting in his murder (Sciolino, 2000).

2. In these two cases, respondents indicated that they were unfamiliar with the Larry Nassar case in one question, but that they were aware of the Larry Nassar case in the next question. There were also other indications in their surveys that they were answering randomly.
3. Specifically, two items in the 'religious intolerance' scale measured whether 'Christians are intolerant of others', and 'Catholics have a "holier than thou" attitude'. These two measures did not load on the scale and were dropped. In addition, the racial intolerance scale included an item indicating whether members of racial minorities should be allowed to rent to buy houses even when the person selling doesn't want to rent or sell to them. This item did not load on the scale with the others and was not included in the final scale.

Disclosure statement

No potential conflict of interest was reported by the authors.

ORCID

Christina DeJong http://orcid.org/0000-0002-7480-164X
Skyler J. Morgan http://orcid.org/0000-0003-0131-6800
Alison Cox http://orcid.org/0000-0002-6511-9905

References

Amnesty International. (2012). *'I wanted to die': Syria's torture survivors speak out*. London: Author.

Anderson, I. (2007). What is a typical rape? Effects of victim and participant gender in female and male rape perception. *British Journal of Social Psychology*, *46*, 225–245.

Aosved, A.C., & Long, P.J. (2006). Co-occurrence of rape myth acceptance, sexism, racism, homophobia, ageism, classism, and religious intolerance. *Sex Roles*, *55*(7), 481–492.

Aosved, A.C., Long, P.J., & Voller, E.K. (2009). Measuring sexism, racism, sexual prejudice, ageism, classism, and religious intolerance: The intolerant schema measure. *Journal of Applied Social Psychology*, *39*(10), 2321–2354.

Bumiller, E. (2011, July 22). Obama ends 'Don't ask, don't tell' policy. New York Times. Retrieved from http://nytimes.com

Burt, D.L., & DeMello, L.R. (2002). Attribution of rape blame as a function of victim gender and sexuality, and perceived similarity to the victim. *Journal of Homosexuality*, *43*(2), 39–57.

Burt, M. (1980). Cultural myths and supports for rape. *Journal of Personality and Social Psychology*, *38* (2), 217–230.

Chapleau, K.M., Oswald, D.L., & Russell, B.L. (2008). Male rape myths: The role of gender, violence, and sexism. *Journal of Interpersonal Violence*, *23*(5), 600–615.

Check, J.V.P., & Malamuth, N.M. (1983). Sex role stereotyping and reactions to depictions of stranger versus acquaintance rape. *Journal of Personality and Social Psychology*, *45*(2), 344–356.

Chynoweth, S. (2017, November 21). Male rape and sexual torture in the Syrian war: 'It is everywhere'. The Guardian. Retrieved from http://www.theguardian.com

Davies, M., Gilston, J., & Rogers, P. (2012). Examining the relationship between male rape myth acceptance, female rape myth acceptance, victim blame, homophobia, gender roles, and ambivalent sexism. *Journal of Interpersonal Violence*, *27*(14), 2807–2823.

Davies, M., & McCartney, S. (2003). Effects of gender and sexuality on judgements of victim blame and rape myth acceptance in a depicted male rape. *Journal of Community & Applied Social Psychology*, *13*(5), 391–398.

Davies, M., Pollard, P., & Archer, J. (2001). The influence of victim gender and sexual orientation on judgments of the victim in a depicted stranger rape. *Violence and Victims*, *16*(6), 607.

Donnelly, D.A., & Kenyon, S. (1996). 'Honey, we don't do men': Gender stereotypes and the provision of services to sexually assaulted males. *Journal of Interpersonal Violence*, *11*(3), 441–448.

Eigenberg, H., & Baro, A. (2003). If you drop the soap in the shower you are on your own: Images of male rape in selected prison movies. *Sexuality & Culture: An Interdisciplinary Quarterly*, *7*(4), 56–89.

Feild, H.S. (1978). Attitudes toward rape: A comparative analysis of police, rapists, crisis counselors, and citizens. *Journal of Personality and Social Psychology*, *36*(2), 156–179.

Fisher, N.L., & Pina, A. (2013). An overview of the literature on female-perpetrated adult male sexual victimization. *Aggression and Violent Behavior*, *18*(1), 54–61.

Ford, T.M., Liwag-McLamb, M.G., & Foley, L.A. (1998). Perceptions of rape based on sex and sexual orientation of victim. *Journal of Social Behavior and Personality*, *13*(2), 253.

Graham, J.W., Olchowski, A.E., & Gilreath, T.D. (2007). How many imputations are really needed? Some practical clarifications of multiple imputation theory. *Prevention Science*, *8*(3), 206–213.

Groth, A.N., & Burgess, A.W. (1980). Male rape: Offenders and victims. *American Journal of Psychiatry*, *137*(7), 806–810.

Herek, G.M. (1993). Sexual orientation and military service: A social science perspective. *American Psychologist*, *48*(5), 538–549.

Jenkins, M.J., & Dambrot, F.H. (1987). The attribution of date rape: Observer's attitudes and sexual experiences and the dating situation. *Journal of Applied Social Psychology*, *17*(10), 875–895.

Jones, T.M., & Sheets, P. (2009). Torture is in the eye of the beholder: Social identity, news coverage, and Abu Ghraib. *Political Communication*, *26*(3), 278–295.

Kapur, A., & Muddell, K. (2016). When no one calls it rape: Addressing sexual violence against men and boys. International Center for Transitional Justice. Retrieved from http://www.ictj.org

Kassing, L.R., Beesley, D., & Frey, L.L. (2005). Gender role conflict, homophobia, age, and education as predictors of male rape myth acceptance. *Journal of Mental Health Counseling*, *27*(4), 311–328.

Krug, E.G., Dahlberg, L.L., Mercy, J.A., Zwi, A.B., & Lozano, R. (2002). *World report on violence and health*. Geneva: World Health Organization.

Kubiak, S.P., Brenner, H., Bybee, D., Campbell, R., & Fedock, G. (2018). Reporting sexual victimization during incarceration: Using ecological theory as a framework to inform and guide future research. *Trauma, Violence & Abuse*, *19*(1), 94–106.

Kupers, T.A. (2005). Toxic masculinity as a barrier to mental health treatment in prison. *Journal of Clinical Psychology*, *61*(6), 713–724.

Lisak, D. (1993). Men as victims: Challenging cultural myths. *Journal of Traumatic Stress*, *6*(4), 577–580.

Lonsway, K.A., & Fitzgerald, L.F. (1995). Attitudinal antecedents of rape myth acceptance: A theoretical and empirical reexamination. *Journal of Personality and Social Psychology*, *68*(4), 704–711.

Man, C.D., & Cronan, J.P. (2001). Forecasting sexual abuse in prison: The prison subculture of masculinity as a backdrop for deliberate indifference. *Journal of Criminal Law and Criminology*, *92*(1), 127–186.

Mason, P. (2006). Prison decayed: Cinematic penal discourse and populism 1995–2005. *Social Semiotics*, *16*(4), 607–626.
Meyer, D. (2004, May 6). Rush: MPs just 'blowing off steam'. Retrieved from http://cbsnews.com.
Nelson, T.S. (2002). *For love of country: Confronting rape and sexual harassment in the U.S. military*. Binghamton, NY: Haworth Press.
O'Brien, C., Keith, J., & Shoemaker, L. (2015). Don't tell: Military culture and male rape. *Psychological Services*, *12*(4), 357–365.
Pino, N.W., & Meier, R.F. (1999). Gender differences in rape reporting. *Sex Roles*, *40*(11), 979–990.
Reitz-Krueger, C.L., Mummert, S.J., & Troupe, S.M. (2017). Real men can't get raped: An examination of gendered rape myths and sexual assault among undergraduates. *Journal of Aggression, Conflict and Peace Research*, *9*(4), 314–323.
Rosenstein, J.E., & Carroll, M.H. (2015). Male rape myths, female rape myths, and intent to intervene as a bystander. *Violence and Gender*, *2*(4), 204–208.
Sable, M.R., Danis, F., Mauzy, D.L., & Gallagher, S.K. (2006). Barriers to reporting sexual assault for women and men: Perspectives of college students. *Journal of American College Health*, *55*(3), 157–162.
Scarce, M. (1997). *Male on male rape: The hidden toll of stigma and shame*. New York: Insight Books.
Sciolino, E. (2000, July 19). Army exonerates officers in slaying of gay private. *New York Times*. Retrieved from http://nytimes.com
Singer, M. (2013). *Prison rape: An American institution?* Santa Barbara, CA: Praeger.
Sivakumaran, S. (2007). Sexual violence against men in armed conflict. *The European Journal of International Law*, *18*(2), 253–276.
Struckman-Johnson, C., & Struckman-Johnson, D. (1992). Acceptance of male rape myths among college men and women. *Sex Roles*, *27*(3/4), 85–100.
Suarez, E., & Gadalla, T.M. (2010). Stop blaming the victim: A meta-analysis on rape myths. *Journal of Interpersonal Violence*, *25*(11), 2010–2035.
Tomlinson, D.R., & Harrison, J. (1998). The management of adult male victims of sexual assault in the GUM clinic: A practical guide. *International Journal of STD & AIDS*, *9*(12), 720–725.
Turchik, J.A., McLean, C., Rafie, S., Hoyt, T., Rosen, C.S., & Kimerling, R. (2013). Perceived barriers to care and provider gender preferences among veteran men who have experienced military sexual trauma: A qualitative analysis. *Psychological Services*, *10*(2), 213–222.
Turhcik, J.A., & Edwards, K.M. (2012). Myths about male rape: A literature review. *Psychology of Men & Masculinity*, *13*(2), 211–226.
United States Department of Defense. (1993). Directive: Qualification standards for enlistment, appointment, and induction. Retrieved from http://biotech.law.msu.edu
United States Supreme Court allows Trump military transgender ban (2019, January 22). BBC News. Retrieved from http://bbc.com
Walfield, S.M. (2018). 'Men cannot be raped': Correlates of male rape myth acceptance. *Journal of Interpersonal Violence*, 088626051881777. (online). doi:10.1177/0886260518817777
'We need to talk about male rape': DR Congo survivor speaks out. (2017, August 3). Retrieved from http://bbc.com
Weisz, A.N., & Black, B.M. (2009). *Programs to reduce teen dating violence and sexual assault: Perspectives on what works*. New York, NY: Columbia University Press.

Appendix A. Male Rape Myth Scenarios

College Context:

Steve is a 21-year-old college student, in the final year of his English degree. He lives in an apartment near campus, and works several evenings a week at the local bookstore. On weekends he enjoys going to bars and the movies. He is also an active member of the university's student government and is a member of the racquetball club.

One evening after work, Steve made his way to his car, which was parked in the nearby parking lot. The surrounding streets were quiet, but as Steve walked through the lot toward his car, a man approached him and asked him for a light. As Steve reached into his pocket for his lighter, the man suddenly grabbed him by the arm, pushing him roughly toward the bushes at the darkened rear of the parking lot.

Steve resisted at first, but the man told him threateningly that he would be very sorry if he did not do what he was told. Steve was very scared as the man forced him to the ground. Still issuing threats, the man then raped him. After the rape the man ran away, leaving Steve lying on the ground, bruised and shaken.

Prison Context:

Steve is a 21-year-old inmate, serving the final year of his sentence for auto theft. After release, he will be living with family members in his hometown. He works several evenings a week at the prison library. On weekends he enjoys reading and watching movies. He is also an active member of the inmate's educational society, and helps others determine how they can complete their degrees.

One evening while closing the library, another inmate entered and asked him when the library opened in the morning. As Steve started to answer, the man suddenly grabbed him by the arm, pushing him roughly toward a dark corner of the library.

Steve resisted at first, but the man told him threateningly that he would be very sorry if he did not do what he was told. Steve was very scared as the man forced him to the ground. Still issuing threats, the man then raped him. After the rape the man ran away, leaving Steve lying on the floor, bruised and shaken.

Military Context:

Steve is 21 years old, and serving the final year of his commitment to the United States Military. After his service ends, he will be living with family members in his hometown. On weekends he enjoys reading and watching movies. He also volunteers on the base library when he has free time.

One evening walking back to the barracks, another soldier approached him and asked him for a light. As Steve started to answer, the man suddenly grabbed him by the arm, pushing him roughly toward a dark area of the base.

Steve resisted at first, but the man told him threateningly that he would be very sorry if he did not do what he was told. Steve was very scared as the man forced him to the ground. Still issuing threats, the man then raped him. After the rape the man ran away, leaving Steve lying on the floor, bruised and shaken.

Conflict Context:

Steve is 21 years old, and lives in a country where rebels have been fighting the government. His life has been hard, but recently he has been able to find work in a local village shop. On weekends he enjoys reading and watching movies.

One evening walking back to his home, a rebel soldier approached him and asked him for a light. As Steve started to answer, the man suddenly grabbed him by the arm, pushing him roughly toward a dark area off the path.

Steve resisted at first, but the man told him threateningly that he would be very sorry if he did not do what he was told. Steve was very scared as the man forced him to the ground. Still issuing threats, the man then raped him. After the rape the man ran away, leaving Steve lying on the floor, bruised and shaken.

Police response to same-sex intimate partner violence in the marriage equality era

Lynn A. Addington

ABSTRACT
Growing research attention is being devoted to intimate partner violence (IPV) involving sexual minority individuals, which is providing insights about prevalence and disclosure patterns. While this work consistently finds that sexual minority IPV victims are reluctant to report to the police, little is known about actual police response to these victims. One unexplored area concerns how growing societal support and legal recognition of same-sex relationships might affect police response to IPV such as arrest. This issue is particularly timely given the U.S. Supreme Court's 2015 decision in *Obergefell v. Hodges* that legalized same-sex marriage. The present study examines police response to IPV involving same-sex couples using arrest data from the National Incident-Based Reporting System (NIBRS). Findings indicate a relationship between legal recognition of same-sex marriage and arrest in IPV cases for both male and female same-sex couples. Implications of these findings for policy and future research are discussed.

Despite the extensive scholarship devoted to studying intimate partner violence (IPV), much less emphasis has been given to sexual minority groups.[1] One review found over a 15-year period (1999–2013) only 3% of published IPV studies considered lesbian, gay, bisexual or trans* (LGBT) individuals (Edwards, Sylaska, & Neal, 2015). While work in this area is growing, more attention is needed as existing research suggests that sexual minorities experience IPV at rates comparable to, if not higher than, heterosexual individuals (Decker, Littleton, & Edwards, 2018; Edwards et al., 2015). Researchers consistently find that sexual minority IPV victims are reluctant to call police (Decker et al., 2018), which is attributed to factors such as long-standing tensions between sexual minority communities and police (Dwyer, 2014) and fears that police will not take seriously IPV involving same-sex partners (Walters & Lippy, 2016). Relatively little is known about actual police response as few studies have explored these cases. Continuing this line of research is needed. A better understanding of current police response can inform policy to support victims and guide culturally sensitive criminal justice programming.

Now is a particularly relevant time to consider police response to IPV involving sexual minority groups in the United States, particularly same-sex couples, given the evolving support for same-sex relationships that culminated in the U.S. Supreme Court's decision in

Obergefell v. Hodges (2015). The *Obergefell* decision legalized same-sex marriage and highlights changing societal views in the United States toward same-sex relationships. Work by the Pew Research Center has tracked societal views since 2001 when the Center first posed questions about support for same-sex marriage. At that time, a majority of American adults (57%) opposed same-sex marriage (Pew Research Center, 2017). By 2011, more Americans supported same-sex marriage than opposed it, and the numbers in support continue to grow (Pew Research Center, 2017).

Given the focus of *Obergefell* on same-sex marriage, it is not surprising that most discussions about its policy implications emphasize marriage equality. The decision also has implications for IPV in terms of equal access for victims to services and protection (Network for Public Health Law, 2019). While these effects are clearest in cases of IPV involving married couples, changes are evident in efforts to incorporate gender-neutral language in IPV policies, programs, and laws to cover non-married partners (Network for Public Health Law, 2019). An open question is whether growing recognition of same-sex relationships might affect police response to same-sex IPV. This question is of interest given previous studies that attribute decisions not to arrest in same-sex IPV cases to police viewing IPV in terms of heterosexual couples and with a heteronormative paradigm where males are aggressors and females are victims (Russell, 2018). A review of current research indicates no study to date has explored the relationship between increasing legal and social support for same-sex partners and arrest.

In addition to addressing this gap in the literature, a better understanding of arrest in cases of IPV involving same-sex couples is needed because the act of an arrest can signal that police view the incident as a crime and acknowledge the victim. This signal of seriousness and belief is particularly important to sexual minority IPV victims who often feel marginalized and not heard (Walters & Lippy, 2016). The present study seeks to contribute to the literature by examining current police responses in the United States with a focus on arrest in cases of same-sex IPV and considering the extent to which support for same-sex relationships might affect this response.

Background

This background section considers the current literature regarding police and IPV involving same-sex couples. To provide a context for this review, the prevalence of same-sex IPV is presented first. Recent research reviews find prevalence rates for IPV involving lesbian and gay individuals can range widely due to inconsistent methods across studies such as the measurement of IPV and the use of non-representative and small samples (Brown & Herman, 2015; Decker et al., 2018). Studies using data from nationally representative samples such as the National Intimate Partner and Sexual Violence Survey (NISVS) find lifetime prevalence rates for serious physical IPV of 29.4% for lesbian women and 16.4% for gay men (Walters, Chen, & Breiding, 2013) and 12-month prevalence rates for psychological and physical IPV of 18.1% for lesbian women and 16.6% for gay men (Addington, 2018).

Given the levels of IPV involving sexual minority victims as well as the short- and long-term repercussions of IPV (see Gehring & Vaske, 2015, for a summary), a growing area of research attention concerns the ways in which victims seek help and services. IPV victims overall (both heterosexual and sexual minority) are more likely to seek help from informal supports like friends than formal ones (Edwards et al., 2015; McCart, Smith, & Sawyer, 2010; Sylaska & Edwards, 2014). In addition, IPV victims across sexual orientation groups tend not to report to police for a number of shared reasons such as feelings of embarrassment, shame, and isolation as well as fears of retaliation by their partner (Brown & Herman, 2015). Sexual minority IPV victims often grapple with additional barriers to reporting. One is an overall mistrust of police by the LGBT community, which is a legacy from the enforcement of criminal laws targeting sexual minorities (Dwyer, 2014). With regard to IPV incidents, many lesbian and gay IPV victims avoid calling the police due to concerns they will encounter discrimination and insensitive responses (Alhusen, Lucea, & Glass, 2010; Walters & Lippy, 2016) as well as perceptions of their IPV experience being discounted as mutual conflict or less serious than heterosexual IPV (Network for Public Law, 2019). Victims who are 'closeted' may have additional fears about being outed if they report to police (Edwards et al., 2015).

Existing research tends to focus on reasons sexual minority IPV victims do not report or seek help from the police. Much less is known about the number of victims who report to police as well as police response when they are contacted (Decker et al., 2018; Edwards et al., 2015). One reason for this omission is that few organizations gather these data. An exception is the National Coalition of Anti-Violence Programs (NCAVP), which collects information on IPV from sexual minority victims who contact an NCAVP member program. In 2017, the NCAVP found 60% of these victims had contact with law enforcement (via reporting by the victim or another person), which was up from 39% in 2016 (NCAVP, 2018). When sexual minority IPV victims do report, research suggests that they find the police unhelpful (Addington, 2018) and their overall experience is negative (Brown & Herman, 2015). In contrast, the NCAVP (2018) finds more diverse experiences with most victims reporting the officer was courteous or indifferent as compared to hostile.

A small group of studies examine law enforcement response to same-sex IPV. The existing work in this area focuses on arrest and uses two methods. One method examines the decision to arrest by vignettes that alter the gender and sexual orientation of the couple (e.g. Franklin, Goodson, & Garza, 2019; Russell, 2018). These studies find that police are less likely to arrest in the case of a same-sex couple. This pattern is consistent even when considering factors that lead to arrest (such as injury and stereotypical victim behavior) (Franklin et al., 2019). Explanations for these decisions include officer's views on LGBT individuals (including homophobia) and agreement with heteronormative paradigms of IPV (Franklin et al., 2019; Russell, 2018).

In contrast to vignettes, the second method directly measures arrest. Only one study to date has examined actual police response as measured by arrests (Pattavina, Hirschel, Buzawa, Faggiani, & Bentley, 2007), and it is described here as it provides the foundation for the current study. Pattavina et al. (2007) examine IPV arrest patterns for opposite- and same-sex couples using police data from the 2000 National Incident-Based Reporting System (NIBRS). They find two factors influence arrest: mandatory arrest laws and offense seriousness. For all couples but same-sex males, mandatory arrest laws predict arrest. Offense seriousness predicts arrest for all couples when simple assault and intimidation incidents are compared, and for all couples but same-sex females when aggravated and simple assault incidents are compared. These findings are widely referenced as they are from the first – and currently only – study to examine arrest patterns for same-sex IPV.

Research Questions

The foregoing discussion highlights the importance of examining IPV involving same-sex couples and the need for continued research regarding arrest in these cases. Two main research questions guide the present study. The first concerns how factors associated with arrest compare across opposite-sex couples (including both male and female victims) and same-sex couples. As this research question updates the work by Pattavina et al. (2007), it is expected that mandatory arrest laws and offense seriousness affect arrest. Specifically, it is hypothesized that the presence of mandatory arrest laws and more serious offenses increase the likelihood of arrest. The second question extends this inquiry to explore how changing societal views (as reflected by legal recognition of same-sex marriage) affect arrests in IPV cases involving same-sex couples. It is expected that a social and legal climate that supports same-sex marriage would challenge heteronormative views of IPV and increase arrests in same-sex IPV cases. Specifically, it is hypothesized the presence of these same-sex marriage policies predicts the likelihood of arrest.

Methodology

Data

To address these research questions, the present study uses data from the Federal Bureau of Investigation's Uniform Crime Reporting System (UCR), which is based on reported crimes that have come to the attention of local and state police. NIBRS is the new format used to collect crime data for the UCR and gathers information at the incident level rather than as an aggregate count, which was the format under the UCR's traditional summary reporting system. The present study uses 2016 NIBRS data, specifically the incident-level data from the Extract Files generated by the National Archive of Criminal Justice Data (National Archive of Criminal Justice Data, 2018). The 2016 NIBRS are the most recent, publicly available year of data.

NIBRS has three primary strengths for the current study. First NIBRS captures the arrest information needed to address the research questions as well as additional relevant details such as victim demographics, intimate partner relationship, and incident characteristics. Second NIBRS gathers these details from a large enough sample size to allow comparisons across opposite- and same-sex intimate partner dyads. Finally, NIBRS data allow for merging additional variables to the file such as information derived from relevant state laws.

While NIBRS provides a large sample of cases and the essential details needed for this study, one caveat is of note regarding its coverage. The FBI is currently in the midst of transitioning the nation to a fully incident-based UCR by 1 January 2021 (FBI, 2016). While an increasing number of states and local agencies are reporting in NIBRS format, these data have yet to achieve full national coverage. In 2016, 35 states contributed NIBRS data and 16 of these states reported all their crime data in NIBRS format.[2] This participation accounted for approximately 37% of law enforcement agencies reporting NIBRS data, which covered about 31% of the population in 2016 (FBI, 2017a).

Case Selection Criteria

To select the eligible cases for this study, the following criteria are used. Incidents are selected if they involve: (1) an aggravated assault, simple assault or intimidation, (2) one victim and one offender, and (3) an intimate partner victim–offender relationship. This study focuses on non-fatal assaultive violence and single victim-offender cases based on previous work that indicates different dynamics may be involved in these incidents as compared to ones involving fatal IPV, multiple victims/offenders or both (Addington & Perueman-Chaney, 2014; Pattavina et al., 2007). Applying these selection criteria results in a final sample size of 297,400 cases.

Within this overall sample, IPV incidents are further categorized by intimate partner dyad: two opposite sex (female victim-male offender and male victim-female offender) and two same sex (female victim-female offender and male victim-male offender). These groups allow comparisons within and across same-sex and opposite-sex couples. Two points are worth noting about the creation of these dyads in terms of sex and victim–offender relationship. First, NIBRS uses a binary (male/female) measure of sex as gender identity information is not currently collected. Second, for purposes of this study, intimate partners are identified by NIBRS victim-offender codes, which include spouse, common law spouse, ex-spouse, and boy/girlfriend as well as 'homosexual relationship'. In 2017, the FBI announced it would discontinue using the homosexual relationship code as a victim–offender relationship option (FBI, 2017b). In 2016, some law enforcement agencies already were using specific intimate partner relationships for same-sex couples. This study includes all relevant intimate partner codes in order to fully capture the eligible IPV cases.

Variables

The following discussion describes the variables used in this study as well as their coding. Appendix A provides the frequencies for the outcome and independent variables.

Outcome variable

Police response is measured as *arrest*. The outcome variable identifies whether the incident involved an arrest. It is a bivariate measure coded as arrest or not.

Independent Variables

This study categorizes independent variables into three groups: individual, situational and legal characteristics. The legal characteristics are the predictors of interest. The variables selected incorporate previous studies described in the Background section including the Pattavina et al. (2007) analysis using 2000 NIBRS data.

Victim characteristics. In addition to considering the victim-offender intimate partner sex dyad, individual characteristics include race. *Race* is coded as white and non-white given the vast majority of IPV incidents involve white victims (Appendix A) as well as the small percentage of victims who are non-Black persons of color and the desire to retain cases for analysis. NIBRS does not consistently collect data on ethnicity as it is not a required data element. As such, Hispanic demographic information is not included in the current study.

Situational characteristics. Situational characteristics include offense seriousness and home location as these are both characteristics associated with arrest. *Offense seriousness* is measured as a type of crime and coded as aggravated assault, simple assault and intimidation. By NIBRS definition of assaultive violence, these offenses include the presence (or absence) of characteristics associated with seriousness such as injury and weapon. As such, specific incident details such as weapon or injury are not included in these analyses given the high correlation with crime type. *Home* location identifies whether the incident occurred in a residence or not. Home location is included as a common location for IPV and as a proxy for possible bystanders or witnesses, which can affect the decision to arrest.

Legal characteristics. Mandatory arrest and same-sex marriage laws are the predictor variables of interest for this study. The NIBRS data file does not include information about state laws so these variables had to be generated from external sources. *Mandatory arrest* identifies whether a state requires police to make an arrest in the case of IPV. The information to create this variable uses the American Bar Association's identification of state IPV arrest laws (American Bar Association, 2014) as well as an independent confirmation of each state's statue. Statutes were coded as mandatory (mandating arrest in all cases of IPV), mixed (mandating arrest only when certain characteristics are present), preferred (preferring arrest but not requiring it), or discretionary (allowing officers to use their discretion). Appendix B provides a list of these codes for the states that contributed 2016 NIBRS data. In the analyses, only states with a clear mandate to arrest in any case of IPV are coded as mandatory arrest states (Appendix A).

The other legal variable identifies '*early adopters*', which are those states that recognized same-sex marriage or unions prior to the *Obergefell* decision. The early adopter variable serves as a proxy measure of a social climate that supports same-sex relationships. An early adopter is a state that recognized same-sex marriages or unions based on its legislation or a state-court decision. States, where same-sex marriage was imposed by a federal district or appellate court, are not included as this situation arguably does not reflect the underlying social climate of the state. The state information to create this variable is based on FindLaw (n.d.).

Analysis

To answer the research questions posed, this study relies on binary logistic regression models. This method is appropriate given that the outcome measure (arrests) is a binary variable. Separate models are estimated for the four intimate partner sex dyads.

Caution is needed when interpreting the results given the large number of cases involved in this study. Since the probability of rejecting the null hypothesis increases with large sample sizes (Lehmann, 2004), it is possible that significance will be found merely due to samples involving thousands of cases. This issue is particularly a concern for the opposite-sex IPV dyad groups (234,944 female victim-male offender cases and 55,729 male victim-female offender cases). While statisticians have devoted a great deal of attention to addressing the issue of very small samples, little attention has been devoted to the best practice for handling very large samples overall or with a focus on NIBRS (but see Addington & Perumean-Chaney, 2014). The current study opts to address this concern in the following way. In addition to reporting statistical significance, the current study reports the marginal effects (computed at the mean) and considers substantive (or clinical) significance as alternatives for interpreting the relationships.

One final issue concerns item missing data (that is, information missing from particular variables). While imputation provides a means of addressing the errors that arise with item missing data, imputation also introduces other forms of error. Only one variable has missing data (victim race) with levels under 2%. This amount of missing data falls within the range where complete case analysis is an acceptable strategy (Allison, 2002).

Findings

Before addressing the research questions, it is useful to consider the bivariate relationships between the study variables and the four intimate partner sex dyads. These descriptive findings provide a context for the characteristics of IPV incidents and identify initial variations across dyads. As indicated in Table 1, many of the bivariate patterns are similar across the intimate partner sex dyads. With regard to the type of offense, the vast majority of incidents involve simple assaults and this pattern is consistent across opposite- and same-sex couples. Incidents involving same-sex male dyads have a slightly higher percentage of aggravated assaults (17.9%) than other dyads. Over half of incidents result in an arrest. A slightly higher percentage of arrests occur in incidents involve male victims (both opposite sex, 59%, and same sex, 56%) than female victims (53% for both dyads). IPV incidents largely and consistently involve white victims with the exception of same-sex female dyads where white and non-white victims are more evenly split than the other dyads (51% to 49%). The vast majority of incidents occur at a home location with opposite-sex dyads having the highest percentage of incidents occurring at home (80% for both male and female victims). About one-third of incidents occur in states with a mandatory arrest law and about a quarter in states that were early adopters of same-sex marriage.

With this context in mind, findings for each research question are reviewed. The first research question considers police response to IPV in terms of arrest and whether

Table 1. Model Variables by Intimate Partner Sex Dyad, 2016 NIBRS.

	Male Victim	Female Victim	Male Victim	Female Victim
	Female Offender	Male Offender	Male Offender	Female Offender
Offense				
Aggravated assault	15.1%	13.0%	17.9%	14.3%
Simple assault	75.3%	73.1%	71.3%	75.2%
Intimidation	9.6%	13.9%	10.8%	10.5%
Arrest Made				
Arrest	59.0%	53.0%	56%	53%
Race				
White	68.3%	67.9%	66.9%	51.0%
Non-White	31.7%	32.1%	33.1%	49.0%
Home Location				
Home	80.6%	80.4%	77.4%	76.6%
IPV Arrest Law				
Mandatory	34.3%	32.7%	35.8%	31.3%
Same-Sex Marriage				
Early adopter	25.4%	22.8%	28.4%	25.5%

characteristics associated with arrest (particularly mandatory arrest laws and offense seriousness) vary across intimate partner dyad. Table 2A and B present the models of IPV incidents involving opposite-sex intimate partner dyads. Table 2C and D present the models for same-sex dyads. All four models are discussed, but the opposite-sex partner dyads are of interest mainly as a context for exploring the same-sex models.

Tables 2A-2D: Binary Logistic Regression Predicting Arrest by Intimate Partner Sex Dyad, 2016 NIBRS.

Table 2A. Female Victim-Male Offender Dyad

Variables	B	se	p value	Odds Ratio (95% CI)	Marginal Effects
Individual					
Race-White	0.6	0.01	<.001	1.82 (1.78-1.85)	0.149
Situational					
Location-Home	0.07	0.01	<.001	1.07 (1.05-1.10)	0.017
Offense					
Aggravated Assault	0.33	0.01	<.001	1.39 (1.36-1.43)	0.080
Intimidation	-1.07	0.1	<.001	0.34 (0.33-0.35)	-0.255
Legal					
Arrest-Mandatory	0.36	0.01	<.001	1.43 (1.41-1.46)	0.089

n = 230,525
note: offense comparison group = simple assault
note: marginal effects computed at mean
Hosmer and Lemeshow Test – Chi-Sq = 131.78 (p<.001)

Table 2B. Male Victim-Female Offender Dyad

Variables	B	se	p value	Odds Ratio (95% CI)	Marginal Effects
Individual					
Race-White	0.4	0.02	<.001	1.49 (1.43-1.54)	0.095
Situational					
Location-Home	0.14	0.02	<.001	1.15 (1.10-1.21)	0.033
Offense					
Aggravated Assault	0.19	0.03	<.001	1.21 (1.15-1.27)	0.043
Intimidation	-1.62	0.03	<.001	0.2 (0.19-0.21)	-0.382
Legal					
Arrest-Mandatory	0.55	0.02	<.001	1.74 (1.67-1.81)	0.130

n = 54,751
note: offense comparison group = simple assault
note: marginal effects computed at mean
Hosmer and Lemeshow Test – Chi-Sq = 21.58 (p<.001)

Table 2C. Female Victim-Female Offender Dyad

Variables	B	se	p value	Odds Ratio (95% CI)	Marginal Effects
Individual					
Race-White	0.49	0.07	<.001	1.64 (1.44-1.87)	0.121
Situational					
Location-Home	0.06	0.08	0.42	1.07 (0.92-1.24)	0.015
Offense					
Aggravated Assault	0.05	0.09	0.56	1.06 (0.88-1.27)	0.012
Intimidation	-1.5	0.12	<.001	0.22 (0.18-0.29)	-0.346
Legal					
Arrest-Mandatory	0.38	0.07	<.001	1.46 (1.27-1.69)	0.094

n = 4,014
note: offense comparison group = simple assault
note: marginal effects computed at mean
Hosmer and Lemeshow Test – Chi-Sq = 3.19 (p = .87)

Table 2D. Male Victim-Male Offender Dyad

Variables	B	se	p value	Odds Ratio (95% CI)	Marginal Effects
Individual					
Race-White	0.65	0.09	<.001	1.91 (1.61-2.29)	0.160
Situational					
Location-Home	0.04	0.1	0.71	1.04 (0.85-1.26)	0.010
Offense					
Aggravated Assault	0.29	0.11	0.01	1.33 (1.07-1.65)	0.070
Intimidation	-1.53	0.15	<.001	0.22 (0.16-0.29)	-0.357
Legal					
Arrest-Mandatory	0.33	0.09	<.001	1.39 (1.17-1.66)	0.081

n = 2,548
note: offense comparison group = simple assault
note: marginal effects computed at mean
Hosmer and Lemeshow Test – Chi-Sq = 2.66 (p = .85)

Turning first to the opposite-sex models, mandatory arrest increases the odds of an arrest for both female victims (OR = 1.43) and male victims (OR = 1.74). Marginal effects provide additional context for this relationship. For female victims, the probability of an arrest is 8.9% higher when there is a mandatory arrest law, and for male victims, this probability is 13% higher.

Examining the opposite-sex models beyond the mandatory arrest predictor, all variables have a statistically significant relationship with arrest (Table 2A and B). The odds of an arrest increase for incidents involving white victims (OR = 1.82 for female victims; 1.49 for males), home locations (OR = 1.07 for female victims; 1.15 for males), and aggravated as compared to simple assaults (OR = 1.39 for female victims; 1.21 for males). The odds of an arrest decrease for incidents involving intimidation rather than simple assault (OR = 0.34 for female victims; 0.2 for males). As noted in the Methods section, one reason for finding statistical significance could be due to the very large sample sizes.[3] The marginal effects provide an additional interpretation and a way to consider the substantive significance. Of all the variables, victim race and intimidation (as compared to simple assault) have the largest marginal effects (in absolute terms) for female and male victims. For female victims (Table 2A), the probability of an arrest is 25.5% lower when the incident involves intimidation as compared to a simple assault and for male victims, the probability of an arrest in these cases is about 38% lower (Table 2B). For female victims, the probability of arrest is almost 15% higher when a white rather than non-white victim is involved; and for males, the probability of arrest is almost 10% higher in these cases. Home locations and aggravated assaults (as compared to simple assaults) have the smallest probabilities. Home location increases the probability of an arrest by less than 2% for female IPV victims and about 3% for male victims. Aggravated assaults (as compared so simple assaults) increase the probability of arrest by 8% for female victims and about 4% for male victims.

Turning to the same-sex intimate partner dyad models (Table 2C and D), a different pattern emerges. For both models, mandatory arrest increases the odds of an arrest (OR = 1.46 for female victims; OR = 1.39 for male victims). The marginal effects for mandatory arrest indicate the probability of an arrest for female same-sex couples is 9.4% higher when there is a mandatory arrest law. For male same-sex partners, the probability of an arrest is 8.1% higher. Considering the other variables, victim race and intimidation have similar relationships to arrest across same-sex models as well as in comparison to the patterns observed in the opposite-sex models. Incidents involving white victims (as compared to non-white victims) increase the odds of an arrest (OR = 1.64 for female victims; OR = 1.91 for male victims). Victim race has a larger probability of predicting arrest than mandatory arrest laws for both female victims (white victims increased the probability of an arrest 12% as compared to non-white victims) and male victims (white victims increased the probability of arrest by 16%). As was the case for opposite-sex couples, intimidation lowers the odds of an arrest (OR = 0.22 for both male and female victims). Intimidation has the largest probability (in absolute terms) of predicting arrest. For both male and female same-sex IPV victims, incidents involving intimidation as compared to simple assault lowered the probability of arrest by 35%. In contrast to opposite-sex models, home location is not associated with an arrest for either female or male same-sex couples (Table 2C and D). Aggravated assault also has a different pattern as compared to the opposite-sex models. For the female same-sex dyad model, arrest did not differ by offense type for aggravated assaults and simple assaults. For the male same-sex dyad model, in comparison, aggravated assaults as compared to simple assaults increase the odds of an arrest (OR = 1.33) and increase the probability by 7%. For both same-sex models, the Hosmer-Lemeshow test indicated that the model is a good fit.

The second question focuses on same-sex couples and explores whether there is a relationship between legal recognition of same-sex marriage and arrest in IPV incidents. Table 3 presents the same-sex female dyad model that includes the early adopter variable. Early adoption of same-sex marriage increases the odds of an arrest (OR = 1.97). The probability of arrest for female same-sex couples is 16.4% higher when the incident occurred in a state that was an early adopter of same-sex marriage as compared to one that was not. Victim race, intimidation incidents and mandatory arrest laws also have a statistically significant relationship with arrest. Mandatory arrest laws also increase the odds of an arrest (OR = 1.21) as do white victims as compared to non-white victims (OR = 1.48). Incidents involving intimidation have a lower odds of arrest as compared to simple assault (OR = 0.23). As was the case with the mandatory arrest model (Table 2C), incidents involving intimidation have the largest probability of arrest (in absolute terms)

Table 3. Binary Logistical Regression Predicting Arrest, 2016 NIBRS Female Victim-Female Offender Dyad.

Variables	B	se	p value	Odds Ratio (95% CI)	Marginal Effects
Individual					
Race – White	0.39	0.07	<.001	1.48 (1.29–1.69)	0.097
Situational					
Location – Home	0.1	0.08	0.19	1.11 (0.95–1.29)	0.025
Offense					
Aggravated Assault	0.04	0.09	0.71	1.04 (0.86–1.25)	0.01
Intimidation	−1.47	0.12	<.001	0.23 (0.18–0.29)	−0.338
Legal					
Arrest – Mandatory	0.19	0.08	0.01	1.21 (1.04–1.40)	0.047
Same sex marriage	0.68	0.09	<.001	1.97 (1.67–2.32)	0.164

n = 4,014
Note: offense comparison group = simple assault
Note: marginal effects computed at mean
Hosmer and Lemeshow Test – Chi-Sq = 3.39 (p =.85)

as they lower the probability of an arrest by about 34%. The probability of arrest is the smallest when considering victim race (9.7% for white versus non-white victims) and mandatory arrest laws (4.7% higher). As observed in the mandatory arrest model, home location and aggravated assault (as compared to simple assault) do not have a statistically significant relationship with arrest for female victims of same-sex IPV. The Hosmer-Lemeshow test suggests the model is a good fit.

Table 4 presents the same-sex male dyad model. As with the same-sex female dyad model, early adoption of same-sex marriage increases the odds of an arrest (OR = 2.69) for same-sex male IPV incidents. The marginal effects indicate the probability of an arrest is 23.1% higher when there was early adoption of same-sex marriage. As was the case with the same-sex female model (Table 3), victim race and intimidation incidents have a statistically significant relationship with arrest. White victims as compared to non-white victims increase the odds of an arrest (OR = 1.66), and intimidations as compared to simple assaults lower the odds of an arrest (OR = 0.23). As was the case with the same-sex female model (Table 3) and the male same-sex mandatory arrest model (Table 2D), intimidation incidents have the largest probability of arrest (in absolute terms) as they lower the probability of arrest by about 34% as compared to simple assaults. Unlike the same-sex female model, the mandatory arrest variable is not statistically significant. Unlike the same-sex female model but consistent with the mandatory arrest model for same-sex male couples, aggravated assaults increase the odds of an arrest (OR = 1.33) and increase the probability of arrest by 7% as compared to simple assaults. As was the case with the mandatory arrest model, home location is not statistically significant. The Hosmer-Lemeshow test suggests the model is a good fit.

Discussion

The present study sought to explore police response in terms of arrest for cases of same-sex IPV. Two primary motivations prompted this work. One was to update the literature regarding arrest and same-sex IPV to better capture current legal and social support for same-sex relationships. A second reason was to provide a framework for future research to support policy concerning same-sex IPV and victim support. Findings from this study

Table 4. Binary Logistical Regression Predicting Arrest, 2016 NIBRS Male Victim-Male Offender Dyad.

Variables	B	se	p value	Odds Ratio (95% CI)	Marginal Effects
Individual					
Race – White	0.51	0.09	<.001	1.66 (1.34–1.99)	0.126
Situational					
Location – Home	0.11	0.1	0.28	1.12 (0.91–1.37)	0.027
Offense					
Aggravated Assault	0.29	0.11	0.01	1.33 (1.07–1.66)	0.07
Intimidation	−1.43	0.15	<.001	0.24 (0.18–0.33)	−0.335
Legal					
Arrest – Mandatory	−0.001	0.1	0.99	1 (0.82–1.21)	−0.001
Same sex marriage	0.68	0.09	<.001	2.69 (2.16–3.33)	0.231
n = 2,548					

Note: offense comparison group = simple assault.
Note: marginal effects computed at mean.
Hosmer and Lemeshow Test – Chi-Sq = 12.38 (p =.10).

contribute to the existing literature by providing this foundational information. These findings are discussed below in the context of the research questions posed and in terms of specific suggestions for future work.

The first question explored predictors of police response to IPV in terms of arrest. Bivariate analyses (Table 1) suggest similar patterns of arrest across dyads with incidents involving male victims having slightly higher arrest percentages for both opposite-sex (59%) and same-sex (56%) couples. When controlling for characteristics related to arrest, mandatory arrest laws have a statistically significant relationship with arrest for all four intimate partner dyads. Mandatory arrest laws, though, do not have the largest probability of predicting arrest. Offense seriousness appears to have the greatest influence on arrest. Intimidation incidents as compared to simple assaults have the largest probability (in absolute terms) of predicting arrest across all four dyads (specifically making an arrest less likely). For both same-sex dyads, victim race also plays a role in IPV response as it has a larger probability of predicting arrest than mandatory arrest laws. These findings suggest that mandatory arrest laws are important to consider when examining arrest for both opposite-sex and same-sex couples, but specific IPV characteristics may play a greater role in this response.

These findings largely confirm the existing research, particularly the Pattavina et al. (2007) study. The main difference is the relationship between mandatory arrest laws and arrest for male same-sex IPV. The present research finds a statistically significant relationship between the two while the previous study did not. Possible explanations for this finding could be due to changes in the law and societal views regarding same-sex relationships as the Pattavina et al. (2007) study relied on 2000 data and the present study uses 2016. Previous research suggests that heteronormative views of IPV that focus on female victims may result in police not arresting in cases of same-sex male IPV (Russell, 2018). Changing views on same-sex relationships might affect these perspectives. A second explanation could be due to participation in NIBRS as more states and law enforcement agencies contributed data in 2016 than in 2000. These additional contributors might reflect different attitudes than the previous contributors. A third explanation could include elements of both changes over time.

Certain differences across dyads are consistent across the current study and the Pattavina et al. (2007) study. These consistent findings highlight areas in need of continued research to understand arrest decisions. One example is the pattern between offense seriousness and arrest in female same-sex IPV cases. Here no statistically significant relationship is observed between aggravated (as compared to simple) assault and arrest. In contrast, this relationship is statistically significant for the other three dyads, which is consistent with expectations from previous research that the likelihood of arrest increases with offense seriousness. Gender-based explanations also might be involved especially for patterns of male victims, in which previous studies of IPV have suggested more serious violence relate to reporting and arrest for IPV and male victims (e.g. Addington & Perumean-Chaney, 2014). Regarding the patterns for female same-sex IPV, paradigms of gender and sexual orientation may be involved in decisions to arrest. The lack of difference in arrest between simple and aggravated assaults might be attributable to implicit bias by police officers regarding views of female-on-female offenses as being less serious overall, whether involving IPV or not (e.g. Weiss, Addington & Nolan, 2018). Exploration of these explanations is beyond the scope of this article. Future work is needed to explore these cases and the officer decision-making process to better understand this pattern.

The second research question explores the effect of growing support for same-sex relationships on IPV arrest. The findings obtained indicate that IPV incidents occurring in states that recognized same-sex marriage prior to the *Obergefell* decision increased the odds of an arrest even when controlling for other factors including mandatory arrest laws. Early adoption of same-sex marriage laws had the largest probability of predicting IPV arrest for both male and female couples with the exception of offense seriousness (intimidation as compared to simple assault). While these findings are preliminary, they suggest the need to further explore this relationship especially given previous studies that connect arrest decisions to police officer agreement with heteronormative views of IPV as well as homophobic beliefs. Future studies could specifically explore whether social and legal recognition of same-sex relationships serve to challenge traditional paradigms of IPV and, in turn, influence police response. In addition, further research is needed to confirm this pattern, especially to investigate whether other characteristics in early-adopter states may be associated with same-sex IPV arrest.

Areas of Future Research to Inform Policy

Although the findings from this study are preliminary, they suggest additional topics for future research that could benefit policy development regarding sexual minority IPV. One concerns a need to broaden the definition of police response as a way to better support victims. A second identifies the need to consider culturally sensitive processing for those arrested. A third reiterates the need to improve the understanding of IPV involving sexual minority individuals.

This study focused on arrest as a measure of police response. Future research should consider additional measures of response, especially ones relevant to sexual minority victims. This research could inform policies that to improve police-victim relationships. For example, an alternative measure could be to focus on response in terms of informing victims about available services, particularly those offered by culturally sensitive service providers. Police can play an important role in connecting victims to services (Warnken & Lauritsen, 2019). Research in this area could identify best practices for disseminating this information to sexual minority victims. Another set of measures could focus on victim satisfaction with the process, which would be useful to explore from a procedural justice perspective. Previous research suggests sexual minority victims report negative experiences with the police. A better understanding of interactions between police and sexual minority IPV victims could identify policy to address these specific complaints and improve relationships with the larger LGBT community.

A second research area concerns IPV offenders. Most work on sexual minority IPV focuses on victims and little is known about offenders (Decker et al., 2018). This study finds that over half of same-sex IPV involve an arrest. This pattern suggests the need for research to explore how these offenders are processed by law enforcement. Such work could identify best practices to ensure culturally sensitive processing of sexual minority offenders.

Finally, this study is limited to same-sex IPV. To fully understand police response to these incidents, research needs to be inclusive of IPV involving all sexual minorities as well as individuals in same-sex relationships that do not identify as a sexual minority.[4] This work is particularly needed for bisexual individuals who are at higher risk for IPV (Addington, 2018; Walters et al., 2013) as well as trans* and genderqueer individuals who are largely unidentified from national collections of crime and victimization data and therefore absent from studies relying on these sources. Reviews of the literature continue to highlight the lack of attention to these IPV victims (Calton, Cattaneo, & Gebhard, 2016; Decker et al., 2018). This omission is largely due to a dearth of available data, which is beginning to change as federal agencies start to include sexual orientation and gender identity questions to their data collections. In addition to efforts at the federal level, IPV research needs to be sensitive to this issue. One way is to consider best practices for inclusive data collection to ensure accurate measurement of sexual orientation and gender identity.

Limitations

While this research provides important initial insights regarding arrest in same-sex IPV cases, it is exploratory and has limitations. The main ones arise from NIBRS and its available measures and current coverage. While NIBRS provides the benefit of a large number of cases to identify same-sex IPV, it has few explanatory variables and no information on the officer or the arrest decision-making process. In addition, NIBRS currently does not directly measure sexual orientation or gender identity. As such, the findings and conclusions drawn also are limited to considerations of same-sex couples and cannot be extended to specific sexual minorities. As mentioned previously, NIBRS currently lacks national coverage. Police departments that do report NIBRS data tend to be mid-size or smaller agencies. A limitation with coverage is that these agencies likely do not have specialized units for domestic violence or LGBT outreach, which could affect the cases reported to police as well as arrest decisions. Despite these limitations, the findings obtained provide important insights given the limited information about the current police response to IPV.

Conclusion

The present study highlights the importance of understanding arrest as a police response to same-sex IPV. Arrests can serve as a signal that police view the incident as a crime and take the victim seriously. This recognition is important to all IPV victims, but particularly sexual minority victims. The findings from this study suggest that evolving views and support for same-sex relationships might influence IPV arrest. While additional work is needed to confirm and explain these findings, they provide a foundation for future research to consider ways to support same-sex IPV victims and assess police response in these cases.

Notes

1. This article opts to use the terms 'victim' and 'intimate partner violence'. Relationship focused terms such as 'same-sex' and 'opposite-sex' couples may be used when the individual's sexual orientation identification is not clear. It is acknowledged that particular areas of scholarship or policy may prefer the use of other terminology (such as 'survivor' rather than 'victim' or 'domestic violence' rather than 'intimate partner violence').

2. Another three states (Alabama, Illinois, and Mississippi) and Washington DC have individual law enforcement agencies that directly send NIBRS data to the FBI based on specific arrangements (FBI, 2017c).
3. The Hosmer-Lemeshow goodness of fit tests for Tables 2A and 2B also are significant, which suggests the models are not a good fit. This finding may be attributable to a large sample size as the test is sensitive to large sample sizes.
4. Compounding this issue is the inaccurate measure of trans* individuals as being in same-sex relationships if they are inaccurately classified based on their sex assigned at birth rather than their gender identity.

Disclosure statement

No potential conflict of interest was reported by the author.

Funding

This project was supported by Award No. 2015-VA-CX-0072, awarded by the National Institute of Justice, Office of Justice Programs, US Department of Justice. The opinions, findings, and conclusions/recommendations expressed in this presentation are those of the author and do not necessarily reflect those of the US Department of Justice.

References

Addington, L.A. (2018). *Using NISVS to explore IPV experienced by lesbian, gay and bisexual individuals.* Annual Meeting of the American Society of Criminology Presentation, Atlanta GA.

Addington, L.A., & Perumean-Chaney, S.E. (2014). Fatal and non-fatal intimate partner violence: What separates the men from the women for victimizations reported to police? *Homicide Studies, 18*(2), 196–220.

Alhusen, J.L., Lucea, M.B., & Glass, N. (2010). Perceptions of and experience with system responses to female same-sex intimate partner violence. *Partner Abuse, 1*(4), 443–462.

Allison, P. (2002). *Missing data*. Thousand Oaks, CA: Sage Publications.

American Bar Association (2014). *Domestic violence arrest policies*. Retrieved from https://www.americanbar.org/content/dam/aba/administrative/domestic_violence1/Charts/migrated_charts/2014_Domestic_Violence_Arrest_Policy_Chart.pdf

Brown, T.N.T., & Herman, J.L. (2015). *Intimate partner violence and sexual abuse among LGBT people: A review of existing research*. Los Angeles, CA: Williams Institute. https://williamsinstitute.law.ucla.edu/wp-content/uploads/Intimate-Partner-Violence-and-Sexual-Abuse-among-LGBT-People.pdf

Calton, J.M., Cattaneo, L.B., & Gebhard, K.T. (2016). Barriers to help seeking for lesbian, gay, bisexual, transgender, and queer survivors of intimate partner violence. *Trauma, Violence, & Abuse, 17*(5), 585–600.

Decker, M., Littleton, H.L., & Edwards, K.M. (2018). An updated review of the literature on LGBTQ+ intimate partner violence. *Current Sexual Health Reports, 10*(4), 265–272.
Dwyer, A. (2014). Pleasures, perversities, and partnerships: The historical emergence of LGBT-police relationships. In D. Peterson & V.R. Panfil (Eds.), *Handbook of LGBT communities, crime, and justice* (pp. 149–164). New York: Springer Science+Business.
Edwards, K.M., Sylaska, K.M., & Neal, A.M. (2015). Intimate partner violence among sexual minority populations: A critical review of the literature and agenda for future research. *Psychology of Violence, 5*(2), 112–121.
Federal Bureau of Investigation. (2016). *The expansion of NIBRS*. Retrieved from https://ucr.fbi.gov/nibrs/2015/resource-pages/the-expansion-of-nibrs-2015_final-1.pdf
Federal Bureau of Investigation (2017a). *Summary of NIBRS 2016*. Retrieved from https://ucr.fbi.gov/nibrs/2016/resource-pages/nibrs-2016_summary.pdf
Federal Bureau of Investigation (2017b). Clarification to policy and procedures. *UCR Program Quarterly (July)*, 6–7. Retrieved from https://ucr.fbi.gov/ucr-program-quarterly/ucr-quarterly-july-2017
Federal Bureau of Investigation (2017c). *Methodology – NIBRS 2016*. Retrieved from https://ucr.fbi.gov/nibrs/2016/resource-pages/methodology-2016_final_.pdf
FindLaw (n.d.). State same-sex marriage laws: A look back. Retrieved from https://family.findlaw.com/marriage/states-that-allow-same-sex-marriage.html.
Franklin, C.A., Goodson, A., & Garza, A.D. (2019). Intimate partner violence among sexual minorities: Predicting police officer arrest decision. *Criminal Justice and Behavior (Online First), 46*(8), 1181–1199.
Gehring, K.S., & Vaske, J.C. (2015). Out in the open: The consequences of intimate partner violence for victims in same-sex and opposite-sex relationships. *Journal of Interpersonal Violence*. doi:10.1177/0886260515600877
Lehmann, E.L. (2004). *Elements of large-sample theory*. New York, NY: Springer.
McCart, M.R., Smith, D.W., & Sawyer, G.K. (2010). Help seeking among victims of crime: A review of the empirical literature. *Journal of Traumatic Stress, 23*(2), 198–206.
National Archive of Criminal Justice Data. (2018). *National incident-based reporting system, 2016: Extract files*. Ann Arbor, MI: Inter-university Consortium for Political and Social Research [distributor]. doi:10.3886/ICPSR37066.v1
National Coalition of Anti-Violence Programs (2018). *Lesbian, gay, bisexual, transgender, queer and HIV-affected hate and intimate partner violence in 2017*. Retrieved from https://avp.org/2017-hv-ipv-report/
Network for Public Health Law (2019). *Issue brief: Status of protections in the U.S. for victims of domestic violence in same-sex relationships*. Retrieved from https://www.networkforphl.org/_asset/9qvjna/Issue-Brief—Status-of-Protections-in-the-U.S.-for-Victims-of-Domestic-Violence-in-Same-Sex-Relationships.pdf
Obergefell v. Hodges (2015), 576 U.S. ___; 135 S.Ct. 1732
Pattavina, A., Hirschel, D., Buzawa, E., Faggiani, D., & Bentley, H. (2007). A comparison of the police response to heterosexual versus same-sex intimate partner violence. *Violence against Women, 13*(4), 374–394.
Pew Research Center. (2017). *Support for same-sex marriage grows, even among groups that had been skeptical*. Retrieved from https://www.people-press.org/wp-content/uploads/sites/4/2017/06/06-26-17-Same-sex-marriage-release.pdf
Russell, B. (2018). Police perceptions in intimate partner violence cases: The influence of gender and sexual orientation. *Journal of Crime and Justice, 41*(2), 193–205.
Sylaska, K.M., & Edwards, K.M. (2014). Disclosure of intimate partner violence to informal social support network members: A review of the literature. *Trauma, Violence, & Abuse, 15*(1), 3–21.
Walters, M.L., Chen, J., & Breiding, M.J. (2013). *The National Intimate Partner and Sexual Violence Survey (NISVS): 2010 findings on victimization by sexual orientation*. Atlanta, GA: Centers for Disease Control and Prevention.

Walters, M.L., & Lippy, C. (2016). Intimate partner violence in LGBT communities. In C.A. Cuevas & C.M. Rennison (Eds.), *The wiley handbook on the psychology of violence* (pp. 695–714). Malden, MA: Wiley & Sons.

Warnken, H., & Lauritsen, J.L. (2019). *Who experiences violent victimization and who accesses services?: Findings from the National Crime Victimization Survey*. Washington, DC: Center for Victim Research.

Weiss, K.G., Addington, L.A., & Nolan, J.J. (2018). Is gender a discretionary factor in reporting and arrests of non-fatal violent crime? *Women & Criminal Justice*, *28*, 1–18.

Appendix A: Study Descriptives

Variable	Frequency	Percentage
Intimate partner sex dyad		
Female victim-Male Offender	234,944	79.0%
Male victim-Female Offender	55,729	18.7%
Female victim-Female Offender	4,101	1.4%
Male victim-Male Offender	2,626	0.9%
Race of victim		
White	197,658	66.5%
Black	87,799	29.5%
Asian	2,969	1.0%
Other	3,412	1.1%
Missing	5,562	1.9%
Offense		
Aggravated assault	39,931	13.4%
Simple assault	218,673	73.5%
Intimidation	38,796	13.0%
Location		
Residence	239,011	80.4%
Other	58,389	19.4%
Arrest		
Yes	161,046	54.2%
No	136,354	45.8%
IPV arrest law		
Mandatory	98,109	33%
Preferred	72,117	24.2%
Mixed	73,058	24.6%
Discretionary	54,116	18.2%
Same-sex marriage early adopter		
Yes	69,650	23.4%
No	227,750	76.6%
n = 297,400		

Appendix B: NIBRS State Characteristics

State*	IPV arrest law	Same sex marriage
Alabama	Discretionary	No
Arizona	Mix	No
Arkansas	Preferred	No
Colorado	Mandatory	Yes
Connecticut	Mandatory	Yes
Delaware	Discretionary	Yes
District of Columbia	Mandatory	Yes
Idaho	Discretionary	No
Illinois	Discretionary	Yes
Indiana	Discretionary	No
Iowa	Mix	Yes
Kansas	Mandatory	No
Kentucky	Discretionary	No
Louisiana	Mandatory	No
Maine	Mandatory	Yes
Massachusetts	Mix	Yes
Michigan	Discretionary	No
Minnesota	Discretionary	Yes
Mississippi	Mandatory	No
Missouri	Mix	No
Montana	Preferred	No
Nebraska	Discretionary	No
New Hampshire	Mix	Yes
North Dakota	Preferred	No
Ohio	Mandatory	No
Oklahoma	Discretionary	No
Oregon	Mandatory	No
Pennsylvania	Discretionary	No
Rhode Island	Mandatory	Yes
South Carolina	Mix	No
South Dakota	Mandatory	No
Tennessee	Preferred	No
Texas	Discretionary	No
Utah	Mandatory	No
Vermont	Discretionary	Yes
Virginia	Mix	No
Washington	Mandatory	Yes
West Virginia	Discretionary	No
Wisconsin	Mandatory	No

*Note not all states are 100% NIBRS reporting

Domestic violence mandatory arrest policies and arrests for same-sex and opposite-sex intimate partner violence after legalization of same-sex marriage in the United States

Alesha Durfee and Leigh Goodmark

ABSTRACT
Historically, legal protection for survivors of intimate partner violence (IPV) in same-sex relationships has been lacking. This changed with the 2015 United States Supreme Court's decision in Obergefell v. Hodges, which invalidated restrictions on same-sex marriage and made legal protections more widely available to survivors of same-sex IPV. In this paper, we analyze the arrest decision in cases of same-sex and opposite-sex IPV using data from the 2016 National Incident-Based Reporting System (NIBRS) – the first year of data post-Obergefell. We also compare our results to previous research and both replicate and extend earlier analyses to see if there are changes in arrest post-Obergefell. Since 1977, states have adopted one of the three types of domestic violence arrest laws: mandatory arrest, pro-arrest, and discretionary arrest. While mandatory arrest laws increase the likelihood of arrest for all and female same-sex couples, they do not have an impact on arrests for male same-sex couples. Pro-arrest laws do not increase the likelihood of arrest for same-sex couples. Finally, the decreased likelihood of arrest when the victim is 'nonwhite' is attributable to the impact of the victim being Black. These results are discussed in the context of previous research on IPV.

Introduction

Researchers first started to look seriously at intimate partner violence (IPV) in same-sex relationships in the late 1980s (see Renzetti, 1997 for review of research). One significant barrier to help-seeking for victims of such violence was the lack of legal protection for and the legal system's hostility towards individuals in same-sex relationships (Richards, Tudor, & Gover, 2018). Protective order laws in many states excluded same-sex partners (Goodmark, 2013). Police, prosecutors, and judges failed to take such violence seriously (Morrison, 2003). Discrimination against individuals in same-sex relationships was permitted as a matter of law (for example, in the denial of marriage licenses and other legal benefits to same-sex partners) (Hunter, 2000).

The social and legal landscape have both changed tremendously since many of the studies on IPV in same-sex relationships were conducted. Public acceptance of same-sex relationships has significantly increased (Pew Research Center, 2019). The United States Supreme Court's decision in Obergefell v. Hodges (2015) invalidated restrictions on same-sex marriage, which both ended legal discrimination in marriage and had collateral benefits for those experiencing IPV in same-sex relationships. Protective order and criminal laws that provided protection to married couples have been extended to those in same-sex marriages. Laws specifically prohibiting individuals in same-sex relationships from obtaining protective orders have been rescinded or overturned (Goodmark, 2020; Richards et al., 2018).

Still, questions persist about the interactions of individuals in same-sex relationships with the criminal legal system. One question involves the operation of mandatory arrest laws in the context of same-sex relationships. Pattavina and colleagues looked at this question in 2007, using data from the 2000 National Incident-Based Reporting System (National Archive of Criminal Justice Data [NACJD], 2009); their findings are summarized below. Given how much has changed since that research was conducted, this paper uses 2016 data to ask similar questions about the impact of arrest policies on arrest rates for IPV in same-sex and opposite-sex relationships, the specific effect of mandatory arrest laws on rates of arrest in same-sex relationships, and changes in those patterns since the 2000 data were collected.

Literature review

Although law enforcement intervention in cases involving IPV has waxed and waned historically, by the 1970s police were routinely failing to make arrests in cases involving IPV (Goodmark, 2012). Discretionary arrest policies, which enabled police to make arrests only when they thought a need to arrest existed, enabled their non-interference. Concerned about this failure to intervene, anti-violence advocates sued police departments for their inaction and sought a way to curb police discretion and force police to arrest those who committed IPV (Gee, 1983; Goodmark, 2018; Houston, 2014). Mandatory arrest laws, which required that police make arrests in cases involving IPV whenever they had probable cause to do so, were seen as a way to ensure police intervention. In 1977, Oregon passed the first mandatory arrest law in the United States (Branch, Khan, & Dretsch, 2018). In 1984, the movement towards mandatory arrest was bolstered by two events. First, Tracey Thurman was awarded millions of dollars when the failure of Torrington, Connecticut police to intervene to protect her from her husband after repeated requests resulted in severe injuries that left her partially paralyzed (*Thurman v. City of Torrington, Connecticut*, 1984). Secondly, Lawrence Sherman and Richard Berk published a study known as the Minneapolis Domestic Violence Experiment, showing that arrest had a deterrent effect on IPV recidivism. Comparing arrest to either ordering one party to leave the premises or advising the parties without making an arrest, Sherman and Berk found that recidivism reduced 50% when suspects were arrested (Sherman & Berk, 1984). Recognizing the potential for liability should police continue their policy of non-interference and armed with Sherman and Berk's research, jurisdictions across the United States adopted mandatory arrest policies.

At the time their research was published, Sherman and Berk warned that the research should be replicated prior to widespread adoption of mandatory arrest policies.

Nonetheless, many jurisdictions quickly moved to adopt such policies. That move was bolstered by requirements in the original iteration of the Violence Against Women Act that states seeking grant monies adopt mandatory arrest requirements (Goodmark, 2018). By 2000, 23 states had adopted mandatory arrest policies (Hirschel, Buzawa, Pattavina, Faggiani, & Reuland, 2007). VAWA was amended in 2003 to require that jurisdictions seeking funding enact either mandatory or pro-arrest policies. Pro-arrest policies express a preference that police make arrests in IPV cases but do not require police to make arrests, even if they have probable cause to do so (Goodmark, 2018). Under pro-arrest policies, police can consider factors including whether the victim wants to arrest and whether police believe the victim is safe in making arrest decisions (Hafemeister, 2011). As of 2016, at least 21 states still had some form of mandatory arrest policy in place, and six had enacted pro-arrest policies.

Researchers have since replicated Sherman and Berk's work in a number of jurisdictions, with varying results (Berk, Campbell, Klap, & Western, 1992; Dunford, Huizinga, & Elliott, 1990; Garner, Fagan, & Maxwell, 1995; Hirschel, Hutchison, & Dean, 1992; Pate & Hamilton, 1992). Metanalyses of these studies have found that arrest for IPV has no significant effect on re-arrest, but may be responsible for lowering rates of revictimization from between 5% and 25% (Maxwell, Garner, & Fagan, 2002; Sugarman & Boney-McCoy, 2000). Arrest rates in IPV cases rose from about 7–15% prior to the inception of mandatory arrest laws to as high as 49% afterwards (Hirschel, Buzawa, Pattavina, & Faggiani, 2007).

The adoption of mandatory arrest policies has had unintended consequences. Perhaps best documented has been the impact of mandatory arrest on arrests of women. Following the adoption of mandatory arrest policies, advocates noted significant increases in arrests of women, both singly and in dual arrests (both parties in the relationship are arrested) (Busch & Rosenberg, 2004; Chesney-Lind, 2002; DeLeon-Granados, Wells, & Binsbacher, 2006; Durfee, 2012; Hirschel & Buzawa, 2002; Miller & Meloy, 2006; Swan & Snow, 2002). Durfee (2012) found that at least part of the increase in arrests of women was 'directly attributable to the implementation of mandatory arrest policies and not simply an increased use of violence by women in intimate relationships' (p.75). Arrests of those identifying as victims of IPV also increased after the inception of mandatory arrest policies (Frye, Haviland, & Rajah, 2007). Those increases continue to be a problem in some places despite the adoption of primary aggressor policies. Such policies are designed to ensure that police ascertain who is primarily responsible for the violence and arrest that person. In a study of 25 jurisdictions, Hirschel and Deveau (2017) found that arrests were 1/3 less likely in states with primary aggressor laws. But Connecticut recently reported that its dual arrest rate is between 18% and 27%, more than twice the national average, despite having adopted a primary aggressor policy (Connecticut Coalition Against Domestic Violence, 2018). Mandatory arrest policies may also depress reporting rates (Dugan, 2003; Novisky & Peralta, 2015; Wolf, Ly, Hobart, & Kernic, 2003). More contested claims about the impact of mandatory arrest include that mandatory arrest laws increase intimate partner homicide (Iyengar, 2009) and that arrest causes premature death of victims (Sherman & Harris, 2015).

Considerably less attention has been paid to the impact of arrest policies on individuals in same-sex relationships. But IPV is a serious problem in same-sex relationships (Branch et al., 2018). IPV is as prevalent in same-sex relationships as in heterosexual relationships (Brown & Herman, 2015). A review of 42 studies on the prevalence of IPV in same-sex relationships found that between 25% and 40% of lesbians had experienced IPV lifetime and 10% had experienced IPV in the last year; approximately 33% of women generally have experienced IPV in their lifetimes, and approximately 4% in the last year (Brown & Herman, 2015). Between 25% and 33% of gay men report IPV in their lifetimes, with around 12% experiencing violence in the past year, compared with a prevalence rate of 28% of men in the general population lifetime and almost 5% in the past year (Brown & Herman, 2015).

While IPV in same-sex and opposite-sex couples shares a number of features, there are dynamics and harms specific to same-sex IPV. Individuals in same-sex relationships may use the fear of disclosure of a partner's sexual orientation to entrap that partner in the relationship. They might undermine a partner by challenging their status as a 'real' man or woman or a 'real' gay man or lesbian or try to convince a partner that no one will believe them about the abuse because they are gay or lesbian (Roe & Jagodinsky, n.d.). Individuals in same-sex relationships may be less likely to recognize what they are experiencing as IPV, to seek outside support, or to receive support when they do seek assistance (Rollè, Giardina, Caldarera, Gerino, & Brustia, 2018). Given that many victim services organizations target their services to heterosexual cisgender women, resources to serve victims of IPV in same-sex relationships are significantly more limited (Girshick, 2002; Rollè et al., 2018).

Researchers have noted that gay and lesbian individuals are particularly vulnerable to arrest (both single and dual) as a result of assumptions and stereotypes that individuals in same-sex relationships are of equal strength and size (and therefore equally culpable for violence in a relationship) (Baker, Buick, Kim, Moniz, & Nava, 2013; Bunker Rohrbaug, 2006). Violence between lesbians is sometimes downplayed because women are thought to be less violent than men or dismissed as a 'catfight' (Hassouneh & Glass, 2008; Ristock, 2002).

Studies have suggested that lesbian and gay individuals experiencing IPV may be reluctant to seek assistance (Rollè et al., 2018), particularly if seeking assistance requires them to interact with police (Kuehnle & Sullivan, 2003; Letellier, 1994; Nadal, Quintanilla, Goswick, & Sriken, 2015; Miles-Johnson, 2013; but see Messinger, 2017). That reluctance may stem from specific fears about police treatment of gay and lesbian victims (Alhusen, Lucea, & Glass, 2010; Parry & O'Neal, 2015) or perceptions that police will not be helpful when responding to calls from individuals in same-sex relationships (Burke, Jordan, & Owen, 2002; Finneran & Stephenson, 2013; Owen, Burke, Few-Demo, & Natwick, 2018). Homophobia and heteronormative misconceptions about IPV affect the police response to same-sex survivors (Franklin, Goodson, & Garza, 2019). A survey by the National Coalition of Anti-Violence Programs found that 47% of LGBTQ survivors who contacted police described police as 'indifferent' towards them; 11% said the police response was 'hostile' (National Coalition of Anti-Violence Programs, 2018, p. 8). The reluctance to contact police may also reflect concerns shared by many victims about 'the legal, financial, and emotional ramifications that police involvement inevitably produces' (Pattavina, Hirschel, Buzawa, Faggiani, & Bentley, 2007, p. 379). Only one study has looked specifically at the impact of mandatory arrest laws on arrests in cases involving same-sex relationships.

Using data from the 2000 National Incident-Based Reporting System Database, Pattavina et al. (2007) found that police made arrests in 50% of cases involving same-sex couples and that same-sex couples were no more or less likely to be arrested than opposite-sex couples. However, in their logistical analysis, mandatory arrest laws increased the likelihood of an arrest in all same-sex relationships and in same-sex female relationships, even after controlling for the type of offense, the race and sex of the victim, and the location of the incident. Pattavina et al. (2007) suggest that societal attitudes which normalize 'low-level' violence for men but not for women may be responsible for these patterns in arrest; it 'takes the passage of a mandatory-arrest law to convince officers that women can be the victims of other women in domestic situations' (p. 388).

Pattavina et al. (2007) also found that the existence of a mandatory arrest policy did not increase the likelihood of arrest for men in same-sex couples. Instead, the type of offense affected the likelihood of arrest for offenders in male same-sex couples, with incidents of aggravated assault more likely, and incidents of intimidation less likely, to result in arrest. Again, these differences may reflect the normalization of 'low-level' violence between men, such that the seriousness of the offense predicted the likelihood of arrest. In addition, incidents with nonwhite victims were less likely to result in arrest for offenders in all same-sex couples, female same-sex couples, and male same-sex couples. Finally, statutory language that explicitly included same-sex couples in mandatory and pro-arrest policies significantly increased the likelihood of arrest for incidents involving male same-sex couples, but not for female same-sex couples.

One of the limitations of Pattavina et al.'s analysis is that only 1,077 of the 176,488 incidents in their study were same-sex couples (0.6%). It is unclear from their paper how many were female versus male same-sex couples. This small sample size likely limited options for how they coded the victim's race, resulting in a dichotomy of white versus nonwhite instead of a more nuanced analysis of victim race and ethnicity. In addition, the legal landscape was significantly different at the time of Pattavina et al.'s study. Same-sex marriage was not legal in the majority of the states. The Defense of Marriage Act (DOMA) precluded the federal government from recognizing same-sex marriages in those jurisdictions where it was legal. Many states did not affirmatively provide protection for or explicitly excluded individuals in same-sex relationships from protection in their criminal and/or protective order laws.

Since Pattavina et al. (2007) conducted their analysis, there have been remarkable changes in the recognition and legal status of same-sex relationships in the United States. Domestic violence arrest law and policy has continued to evolve, with jurisdictions moving between mandatory arrest, pro-arrest, and discretionary arrest laws or policies. Police training in regard to domestic violence, especially in jurisdictions that have adopted lethality assessment programs (Messing et al., 2014), has increased, and the creation of police liaisons to the LGBT community has been linked with greater reporting of IPV in same-sex relationships in some jurisdictions (Colvin, 2012). The number of incidents of IPV (Alhusen et al., 2010) that involve same-sex couples has also increased. In this paper, we replicate and extend Pattavina et al.'s analysis, focusing on the following research questions:

(1) What are the arrest rates for IPV reported to law enforcement in the United States in 2016 for same-sex, opposite-sex, female same-sex, and male same-sex couples? What are the arrest rates by arrest policy, offense type, victim race/ethnicity, victim sex (as recorded by the responding officer(s)), location, victim age, and injuries to

the victim (as recorded by the responding officer(s))? Are there significant differences between same-sex and opposite-sex couples when we look at the impact of these factors individually? For female and male same-sex couples?

(2) Have patterns of arrest for IPV in incidents involving same-sex and opposite-sex couples in the United States changed between 2000 and 2016?

(3) Do mandatory and pro-arrest policies increase the likelihood that an offender in a same-sex relationship will be arrested?

(4) Given that all of the factors listed in research question #1 likely have complex and interconnected relationships to arrests for IPV, once we control for all of these factors, are there differences between same-sex couples and opposite-sex couples in which variables predict arrest? What about for female and male same-sex couples?

Data and methods

For our analysis, we use the 2016 National Incident-Based Reporting System (NIBRS) Victim Extract (NACJD, 2018), which contains a total of 5,951,120 incidents of crime reported to law enforcement. The unit of analysis for the Victim Extract is the victim. We use the 2016 data to analyze arrests for same-sex IPV and to compare patterns of arrest for same-sex and opposite-sex IPV. The 2016 data set provides the first full year of data after the legalization of same-sex marriage (26 June 2015) in the United States. The NIBRS includes individual level detailed information on the demographic characteristics of the victim, offender, and arrestee, circumstances of the incidents, the jurisdiction where the incident took place, and whether (and how) an arrest was made. As of 2016, 39 states (representing about 37% of law enforcement agencies in the US) contributed to the 2016 NIBRS (Federal Bureau of Investigation [FBI], 2017). However, it is important to note that not all jurisdictions in these 39 states participated in the 2016 NIBRS (the goal is for universal reporting in 2021; see FBI, n.d.). A listing of all 39 states included in this analysis, along with their arrest policy type, can be found in Table 1.

Sample

The sample consists of all cases in the NIBRS Victim Extract that have a single adult victim and single adult offender who (1) have an intimate relationship (a spouse, common-law spouse, ex-spouse, boyfriend/girlfriend, or a 'homosexual relationship') and (2) where an act of IPV is listed as an offense. For this paper, we use the definition of IPV employed by Pattavina et al. (2007), which was limited to aggravated assault, simple assault, or intimidation. A hierarchy was imposed on offense to reflect the most serious offense listed for the incident. Sexual violence and kidnapping, although acts of IPV, are not included in our analysis because (1) we wanted to compare patterns of arrest found in 2016 with those in 2000, (2) in the 2016 data, there are relatively few acts of sexual violence among female (n = 10) and male (n = 48) same-sex couples, and (3) it is not possible to place sexual violence on the hierarchy used here to categorize the most serious offense. We then removed all incidents with missing values for the victims' sex and race and the offenders' sex and race (n = 13,580 or 4.5% of the sample), to ensure that

Table 1. Type of domestic violence arrest provisions by state, 2016 (39 states).

Mandatory (n = 18)	Preferred (n = 6)	Discretionary (n = 15)
Arizona	Arkansas	Alabama
Colorado	Massachusetts	Delaware
Connecticut	Michigan	Idaho
Washington, D.C.	Montana	Illinois
Iowa*	North Dakota	Indiana
Kansas	Tennessee	Kentucky
Louisiana		Minnesota
Maine		Missouri
Mississippi		Nebraska
Ohio		New Hampshire
Oregon		Oklahoma
Rhode Island*		Pennsylvania
South Carolina		Texas
South Dakota		Vermont
Utah		West Virginia
Virginia		
Washington		
Wisconsin		

Notes: *Incidents in Iowa and Rhode Island were coded as either mandatory and discretionary arrest due to the complexity of their legal statutes (see Iowa Code Ann. §§ 236.12 (2)(a) and R.I. Gen. Laws § 12–29-3 (b), (c), where mandatory arrest only applies in select incidents).

we had a consistent sample across model types. After imposing these restrictions, the final sample size was 282,168 incidents of IPV.

Dependent variable

Table 2 contains the descriptive statistics for the dependent and independent variables included in this analysis. The dependent variable used for all models is whether the offender was arrested for IPV. Arrest includes the offender being taken into custody, an on-view arrest, or the offender receiving a summons or citation. As Table 1 shows, an arrest for IPV was made in 52% of the cases in the full sample, 53% of cases involving same-sex couples, 52% of cases involving opposite-sex couples, 51% in cases with female same-sex couples, and 54% in cases of male same-sex couples.

Independent variables

The independent variables are described below, and their means and standard deviations are presented in Table 2. Due to the categorical nature of many of the variables, and the requirements of logistic regression, they are coded dichotomously (1 = yes, 0 = no) unless otherwise indicated. For categorical variables with multiple categories, a reference category was created for comparison purposes. As they are dichotomous 0/1 variables, the mean is also the percentage of cases that are a 'yes' for that category. For example, the mean for 'arrest' for the full sample is .52 (see Table 1), which indicates that 52% of the incidents in the full sample resulted in the arrest of the offender.

Table 2. Demographic characteristics of female same-sex, male same-sex, and opposite-sex samples, NIBRS 2016 (N = 282,168).

	Full sample N = 282,168	All same-sex n = 6,276		Opposite-sex n = 275,892	Male same-sex n = 2,461		Female same-sex n = 3,815
Variable	Mean (sd)	Mean (sd)	Hedges's g[2]	Mean (sd)	Mean (sd)	Hedges's g	Mean (sd)
Offender arrested	.52 (.50)	.53 (.50)	−.02	.52 (.50)	.54 (.50)*	.06	.51 (.50)
Arrest policy	.48 (.50).35	.45 (.50)***.39	.07	.48 (.50).34	.45 (.50)*.39	.03	.44 (.50).39
Mandatory	(.48).17	(.49)***.16	-.10.03	(.48).18	(.49).16	-.01	(.49).17
Pro	(.38)	(.39)*		(.38)	(.36)	-.03	(.37)
Discretionary[1]							
Offense type	.13 (.34).74	.16 (.37)***.74	−.08	.13 (.34).74	.16 (.36)***.72	.10	.15 (.35).75
Aggravated	(.44).13	(.44).10	-.00.08	(.44).13	(.45)***.13	-.10.02	(.43).10
assault	(.34)	(.30)***		(.34)	(.34)		(.30)
Simple assault[1]							
Intimidation							
Victim race/	.60 (.50).30	.50 (.50)***.41	.21	.60 (.49).30	.59 (.49)***.32	.29	.44 (.50).47
ethnicity	(.49).08	(.49)***.07	-.25.02.03	(.46).08	(.47)***.08	-.31.06	(.50).07
White[1]	(.27).02	(.26).02		(.27).02	(.28)*.01	-.04	(.25).02
Black	(.15)	(.13)*		(.15)	(.12)		(.14)
Hispanic							
Other							
Victim sex	.80 (.40).20	.61 (.49)***.39	.50	.81 (.00).19	–	–	–
Female[1]	(.40)	(.49)***	-.50	(.00)	–	–	–
Male							
Location	.81 (.39)	.77 (.42)***	.08	.81 (.39)	.78 (.41)	.02	.77 (.42)
Victim age	34.08 (11.23)	31.55 (10.47)***	.23	34.13 (11.45)	34.14 (11.45)***	.29	30.35 (9.60)
Injuries to victim	.46 (.50).51	.39 (.49)***.56	.13	.46 (.50).51	.38 (.48).57	−.06.03.08	.41 (.49).56
No injury[1]	(.50).04	(.50)***.04	-.11	(.50).03	(.50).05		(.50).04
'Minor' injury	(.19)	(.21)**	-.04	(.19)	(.23)		(.19)
'Major' injury							

Notes: [1]reference category. [2]Corrected Hedges's g. *p ≤ .05, **p ≤ .01,***p ≤ .001 for 2-sample *t*-test (same-sex couples vs. opposite-sex couples, female couples vs. male same-sex couples). The mean is the percentage for 0 = no/1 = yes variables.

Type of relationship

We use the terms 'same sex,' 'female same sex,' 'male same sex,' and 'opposite sex' to describe the relationships included here, rather than 'lesbian,' 'gay,' or 'heterosexual,' as the NIBRS does not include information on the sexual orientation of the victim and offender. A relationship that is opposite sex may not be a heterosexual relationship but between two bisexual individuals who happen to be in an opposite-sex relationship. Similarly, females in a same-sex relationship may not identify as lesbian, and males in a same-sex relationship may not identify as gay. Our identification of relationship type comes from the sex categorization of both the victim and offender, and thus it is most appropriate to describe and label them in those terms.

We are limited to the four categories listed above because of the inadequacies of the NIBRS in capturing relationship information for same-sex couples. While other analyses of opposite-sex IPV can examine different types of relationships between the victim and offender, analyses of same-sex IPV are far more limited because NIBRS uses a category called 'homosexual relationship' for the variable capturing the relationship between the victim and offender. The term 'homosexual' is a 'outdated clinical term considered derogatory and offensive,' and 'the Associated Press, New York Times, and Washington Post restrict usage of this term' (GLAAD, n.d.). As the majority of the same-sex relationships in the sample were coded as 'homosexual relationship' (99%) instead of by the more complex relationship types for opposite-sex couples, we are unable to compare arrest rates or officer decision-making between spouses, common-law spouses, ex-spouses, and boyfriend/girlfriends for same-sex couples. Some same-sex relationships in the 2016 NIBRS are instead coded as spouse (n = 51), ex-spouse (n = 6), and boyfriend/girlfriend (n = 21). Thus, we identified same-sex and opposite-sex partnerships by comparing the sex of the victim and the offender as noted by the officer.

Of the 282,168 incidents in the full sample, 6,276 (2.2%) were between same-sex partners, 275,892 (97.8%) between opposite-sex partners, 3,815 (1.4%) between same-sex female partners, and 2,461 (0.9%) between male same-sex partners. This represents a remarkable increase in the *proportion* of incidents of IPV reported to police that involves same-sex partners since the 2000 NIBRS (only 0.6% of their sample were same-sex incidents as compared to 2.2% in the 2016 NIBRS; they do not provide a disaggregated number of female same-sex versus male same-sex incidents in their paper). The increase in total sample size may be due to the increase in the number of states participating in the NIBRS between 2000, when only 19 states participated, and 2016, when 39 states participated. The substantial increase in the number and proportion of same-sex couples in the 2016 sample as compared to the 2000 sample may be due to increased awareness and acceptance of same-sex relationships in 2016 or the proportion of same-sex relationships in the 19 states added to the NIBRS between 2000 and 2016.

State domestic violence arrest policy

The state domestic violence arrest policy reflects the policy adopted by the state in 2016 and includes mandatory arrest, pro-arrest, and discretionary arrest. Arrest policies of each state contributing to NIBRS in 2016 were located using online legal research databases and state statutory compilations. Mandatory arrest policies require officers to make an arrest when they believe an act of domestic violence has occurred. Pro-arrest policies state that arrest is the preferred, but not required, option. Discretionary arrest allows for warrantless arrests in cases of domestic violence but leaves arrest up to the officer's discretion. Individual jurisdictions may have stronger arrest policies than the state arrest policy, but may not adopt weaker ones. Therefore, all jurisdictions in a mandatory arrest state must have mandatory arrest policies; jurisdictions in a pro-arrest or discretionary arrest state may adopt mandatory arrest policies.

As shown in Table 1, 18 states (46%) included in the NIBRS had mandatory arrest, 6 (15%) had pro-arrest, and 15 (38%) had discretionary arrest policies for domestic violence. Two states – Iowa and Rhode Island – had mandatory arrest policies that only applied if there was 'physical injury' to the victim (Iowa Code Ann. §§ 236.12 (2)(a)) or 'felonious assault, assault resulting in injury (physical pain, illness, or an impairment of physical condition), (or) action intending to cause fear of imminent serious bodily injury or death' (R.I. Gen. Laws § 12–29-3 (b), (c)). Given that offenses coded as intimidation might not meet the standards for mandatory arrest, any offenses of intimidation in those states were coded as discretionary arrest. Of the incidents analyzed in this paper, 47% occurred in mandatory arrest, 32% occurred in pro-arrest, and 20% occurred in discretionary arrest states.

Most serious IPV offense

While 92% of incidents had only one offense, 8% of incidents involved between two and five offenses. For cases with more than one offense, we imposed a hierarchy reflecting the relative seriousness of the crime. Any incident that included an offense of aggravated assault was coded as an aggravated assault. Of the remaining cases, any incident that included a simple assault offense was coded as a simple assault. Due to sample selection criteria, all remaining uncategorized cases were coded as acts of intimidation. For the full sample, 13% of incidents were aggravated assaults, 74% were simple assaults, and 13% were acts of intimidation.

Victim race/ethnicity

Victim race and ethnicity were included in the models as a single variable. As we are comparing our results to those of Pattavina et al. (2007), we coded this variable in two different ways (one to match their analysis and a more comprehensive one for our own analysis) and used only victim race/ethnicity (and not offender race/ethnicity). For the first set of analyses (Tables 4 and 5), we coded victim race and ethnicity as a single variable to match that used by Pattavina et al.: 1 for nonwhite and 0 for white. For the expanded models (Tables 6 and 7), victim race and ethnicity were coded as white (the reference category), Black, Hispanic, and 'Other' (Native American, Asian, and Pacific Islander and Native Hawaiian, which were not included as separate categories as too few female and male same-sex couples were of these races to include them as separate categories). White Hispanics were coded as Hispanic, while Black Hispanics were coded as Black, and 'Other' Hispanics were coded as 'Other.' Of the full sample, 60% were white, 30% were Black, 8% were Hispanic, and 2% were 'Other.'

Victim sex

The NIBRS data are limited in that victim sex is observed and categorized by the officer, contain only two biologically based categories ('female' and 'male'), and likely reflect legal status (for example, as represented on state-issued documents like driver's licenses) rather than gender identity. We use victim sex, rather than offender sex, in order to be consistent with the modeling of Pattavina et al. Additionally, because of the way we structured the models, offender sex is predetermined once victim sex is included in the models. For opposite-sex couples, if the victim is female the offender must be male. For same-sex couples, the sex of the victim must be the same as that of the offender. Eighty percent of the incidents in the full sample have female victims and 20% have male victims.

Location of incident

In accordance with Pattavina et al., the location of the incident is categorized by home (1) or all other locations (0). Eighty-one percent of the incidents in the full sample occurred at the victim's residence.

Victim age

The age of the victim is included in the models and is coded as a continuous variable that ranges from 18 to 99. The average age of victims in the full sample is 34.08 years. We did not include offender age as it is highly correlated with victim age and does not improve the prediction of the likelihood of arrest of the offender for IPV. Pattavina et al. also did not include offender age.

Injuries to the victim

Victim injuries are those that are observed by the officer and include 'no injury,' 'minor injury,' and 'major injury.' While 'no injury' and 'apparent minor injury' are classifications used by the NIBRS, we collapsed the NIBRS categories of 'apparent broken bones,' 'other major injury,' 'possible internal injury,' 'loss of teeth,' 'severe laceration,' and 'unconsciousness' into the category of 'major injury.' For the full sample, 46% had 'no injury,' 51% had at least one 'minor injury,' and 4% had at least one 'major injury' observed and noted by the officer. If both minor and major injuries were observed, it was coded as major injury.

Analytic technique

To compare patterns of arrest for IPV between 2000 to 2016 for incidents with same-sex and opposite-sex couples, as well as female and male same-sex couples, we conducted a series of univariate analyses, bivariate analyses, *t*-tests, and logistic regressions. The univariate analyses are included in Table 1 and show the means and standard deviations of the dependent and independent variables used in this analysis. *T*-tests were then conducted to compare the means of all variables between same-sex incidents and opposite-sex incidents and female same-sex couples and male same-sex couples, the results of which are also shown in Table 1. Table 1 also shows the results of the two-sample *t*-tests, the level of significance for the p values, and effect sizes using Hedges's g for comparing the female and male same-sex samples (which are roughly the same size) and a corrected Hedges's g for comparing the same sex and opposite samples (which have very different sample sizes) (Lakens, 2013).

Next, arrest rates were calculated for the full sample and the four sub-samples by arrest policy type, offense type, victim demographics, location, and victim injuries observed (Table 3). Again, two-sample *t*-tests were conducted to see if there were statistically significant differences in arrest rates between the four sub-samples. These results, along with the significance levels for the p values, are also included in Table 3.

Additionally, we conducted a series of logistic regressions identical to Pattavina et al. to determine if any differences in the patterns of arrest rates emerged between 2000 and 2016 (Tables 4 and 5). Differences between our analysis and Pattavina et al.'s are noted in these tables. The odds ratios, the level of significance for the p values, and the 95% confidence intervals are included in Tables 4 and 5.

Finally, because of the increased sample size in the 2016 data, we were able to conduct a series of logistic regressions predicting arrest with a more extensive model that includes a more nuanced measure of victim race/ethnicity and victim's observed injuries (Tables 6 and 7). Other models including measures of weapon use, firearm use, and offender demographics were tested but are not included here as the pattern of effects was unchanged, the additional independent variables did not achieve statistical significance, and there were no changes to the amount of variance in arrest explained by the other models. As in Tables 4 and 5, the odds ratios, the level of significance for the p values, and the 95% confidence intervals are included in Tables 6 and 7.

Table 3. Arrest rates by arrest policy type, offense type, victim demographics, location, and victim injuries observed (N = 282,168).

	Full sample N = 282,168	All same-sex n = 6,276		Opposite-sex n = 275,892	Male same-sex n = 2,461		Female same-sex n = 3,815
Variable	% arrested	% arrested	Hedges's g^2	% arrested	% arrested	Hedges's g^2	% arrested
Arrest policy	54%	56%*	–.04.01	54%	58%	.07.05.04	55%
Mandatory	49%	49%	-.05	49%	50%		48%
Pro	50%	52%		50%	53%		52%
Discretionary[1]							
Offense type	59%	58%	.04	60%	61%*	.13.05.02	55%
Aggravated	54%	56%	-.03.14	54%	57%		55%
assault	27%	21%		28%	22%		21%
Simple assault[1]		***					
Intimidation							
Victim race/	56%	59%**	–.05	56%	59%	.02	58%
ethnicity	41%	44%	-.07	41%	44%	-.02.12	45%
White[1]	57%	***	-.03.15	56%	61%	-.15	55%
Black	62%	58%		62%	50%		58%
Hispanic		55%					
Other							
Victim sex	50%	51%	–.02.06	50%	–	–	–
Female[1]	57%	54%**		57%	–	–	–
Male							
Location	52%	53%	–.02	52%	55%*	.06.05	52%
Home	49%	51%	-.04	49%	49%		50%
Elsewhere[1]							
Injuries to victim	39%	37%*	.05	39%	36%	–.03.08.19	37%
No injury[1]	62%	63%	-.01	62%	65%*		61%
'Minor' injury	64%	65%	-.02	64%	69%		60%
'Major' injury							

Notes: [1]reference category. [2]Corrected Hedges's g. *p ≤ .05, **p ≤ .01,***p ≤ .001 for 2-sample *t*-test (same-sex couples vs. opposite-sex couples, female couples vs. male same-sex couples).

Table 4. Logistic regressions predicting arrest for IPV among same-sex couples replicating Pattavina et al. (2007) with 2016 NIBRS data (n = 6,276).

	All same-sex n = 6,276		Male same-sex n = 2,461		Female same-sex n = 3,815	
Variable	OR (SE)	95% CI	OR (SE)	95% CI	OR (SE)	95% CI
Mandatory arrest	1.28 (.07)***	1.16–1.42	1.34 (.11)***	1.13–1.58	1.25 (.08)***	1.10–1.43
Offense type	1.15 (.08).21	.99–1.32.17 –.25	1.26 (.14)*.20	1.02–1.57.15 –.27	1.07 (.10).21	.89–1.29.16 –.28
Aggravated	(.02)***		(.03)***		(.03)***	
assault						
Intimidation						
Victim nonwhite	.62 (.03)***	.55 –.68	.61 (.05)***	.51 –.72	.62 (.04)***	.54 –.71
Victim male	1.05 (.06)	.95–1.17	–	–	–	–
Location	1.02 (.06)	.90–1.15	1.00 (.10)	.82–1.22	1.03 (.08)	.88–1.20
Constant	1.38 (.10)***	1.20–1.60	1.44 (.16)***	1.16–1.79	1.40 (.13)***	1.18–1.67
Pseudo R^2	.05		.05		.04	

Notes: *p ≤ .05, **p ≤ .01,***p ≤ .001.

Results

According to Table 2, after the legalization of same-sex marriage offenders in same-sex and opposite-sex couples are equally likely to be arrested for IPV (53% and 52%, respectively). However, incidents between male same-sex couples are significantly more likely to result in arrest (54%) than are incidents between female same-sex couples (51%). The

Table 5. Logistic regressions predicting arrest for IPV among opposite-sex couples, replicating Pattavina et al. (2007) with 2016 NIBRS data (n = 275,892).

	All opposite-sex n = 275,892		Opposite-sex with male victim n = 53,083		Opposite-sex with female victim n = 222,809	
Variable	OR (SE)	95% CI	OR (SE)	95% CI	OR (SE)	95% CI
Mandatory arrest	1.25 (.01) ***	1.23–1.27	1.30 (.02) ***	1.25–1.35	1.24 (.01) ***	1.22–1.26
Offense type Aggravated assault Intimidation	1.27 (.01) ***.31 (.00)***	1.24–1.30.30 –.32	1.17 (.03) ***.21 (.01)***	1.11–1.23.19 –.22	1.29 (.02) ***.33 (.00)***	1.26–1.32.32 –.34
Victim nonwhite	.63 (.01)***	.62 –.64	.72 (.01)***	.69 –.75	.62 (.01)***	.60 –.63
Victim male	1.27 (.01) ***	1.24–1.29	–	–	–	–
Location	1.09 (.01) ***	1.07–1.11	1.15 (.03) ***	1.10–1.21	1.08 (.01) ***	1.06–1.11
Constant	1.14 (.01) ***	1.12–1.17	1.35 (.03) ***	1.29–1.42	1.16 (.01) ***	1.13–1.19
Pseudo R^2	.04		.04		.04	

Notes: *p ≤ .05, **p ≤.01,***p ≤ .001.

remainder of the table describes the sample and subsamples. All of the differences described in the next two sections were statistically significant (see Table 2 for the p values and effect sizes).

Same-sex versus opposite-sex couples

Same-sex couples are less likely to live in states with mandatory arrest policies (45%) and discretionary arrest policies (16%) than are opposite-sex couples (48% and 18%, respectively). However, a greater proportion of same-sex couples live in pro-arrest states (39%) than is true for opposite-sex couples (34%). There are also more aggravated assaults among same-sex couples (16%), and fewer incidents of intimidation (10%) reported to law enforcement than for opposite-sex couples (13% and 13%). Victims in the same-sex sample are less likely to be white (50%), more likely to be Black (41%), and less likely to be of another race (2%) than opposite-sex couples (60%, 30%, and 2%). Victims in same-sex couples, on average, are younger (32 years old), less likely to be female (61%) and more likely to be male (39%) than opposite-sex couples (34 years old, 81%, and 19%). Finally, the victims in the same-sex sample are more likely to have minor injuries (56%) and major injuries (4%) than the victims in the opposite-sex sample (51% and 3%).

Female same-sex couples versus male same-sex couples

There are more aggravated assaults among male same-sex couples (16%) than female same-sex couples (15%). Victims in female same-sex couples are, on average, younger (30 years old), less likely to be white (44%), more likely to be Black (47%), and less likely to be Hispanic (7%) than victims in male same-sex couples (34 years old, 59%, 32%, and 8%). Victims in female same-sex relationships are more likely to have officers determine there was 'no injury' (41%) or major injuries (4%) than victims in male same-sex relationships (38% and 5%).

Table 6. Logistic regressions predicting arrest for IPV among same-sex couples; expansion of Pattavina et al. (2007) (n = 6, p. 276).

	All same-sex n = 6,276		Male same-sex n = 2,461		Female same-sex n = 3,815	
Variable	OR (SE)	95% CI	OR (SE)	95% CI	OR (SE)	95% CI
Arrest policy	1.26 (.10)**	1.08–1.46.87–1.18	1.28 (.16)	1.00–1.64.79–1.30	1.24 (.12)*	1.02–1.49.83–1.23
Mandatory arrest	1.01 (.08)		1.01 (.13)		1.01 (.10)	
Pro-arrest						
Offense type	1.07 (.09).36 (.04)***	.91–1.27.29 –.44	1.17 (.15).39 (.07)***	.91–1.52.28 –.55	1.02 (.11).34 (.05)***	.82–1.26.26 –.45
Aggravated assault						
Intimidation						
Victim race/ethnicity	.60 (.04)***.90 (.10).79 (.16)	.53 –.67.73–1.11.54–1.18	.59 (.06)***	.49 –.71.73–1.38.35–1.39	.60 (.04)***.83 (.12).87 (.21)	.52 –.69.63–1.10.54–1.40
Black			1.00 (.16).69 (.25)			
Hispanic						
Other						
Victim male	1.00 (.06)	.90–1.11	–	–	–	–
Location	1.01 (.00)	.89–1.15	1.01 (.11)	.82–1.24	1.01 (.08)	.86–1.19
Victim age	1.00 (.00)	1.00–1.01	1.01 (.00)*	1.00–1.02	1.00 (.00)	.99–1.01
Injuries to victim	2.26 (.13)***	2.01–2.54	2.61 (.26)***	2.15–3.17	2.10 (.16)***	1.81–2.43
'Minor' injury	2.30 (.35)***	1.70–3.10	2.82 (.66)***	1.79–4.45	1.97 (.41)***	1.32–2.95
'Major' injury						
Constant	.70 (.09)**	.54 –.91	.54 (.11)**	.35 –.80	.83 (.14)	.61–1.18
Pseudo R^2	.07		.09		.07	

Notes: *p ≤ .05, **p ≤ .01,***p ≤ .001.

Table 7. Logistic regressions predicting arrest for IPV among opposite-sex couples; expansion of Pattavina et al. (2007) (n = 275,892).

	All opposite-sex n = 275,892		Opposite-sex with male victim n = 53,083		Opposite-sex with female victim n = 222,809	
Variable	OR (SE)	95% CI	OR (SE)	95% CI	OR (SE)	95% CI
Arrest policy	1.31 (.01)	1.29–1.34	1.44 (.04)	1.37–1.52	1.29 (.02)	1.26–1.32
Mandatory	***	1.09–1.14	***	1.16–1.29	***	1.06–1.12
arrest	1.11 (.01)		1.23 (.03)		1.09 (.01)	
Pro-arrest	***		***		**	
Offense type	1.19 (.02)	1.16–1.23.47 –.50	1.12 (.03)	1.06–1.19.34 –.39	1.21 (.01)	1.17–1.24.49 –.52
Aggravated	***.49		***.36		***.51	
assault	(.01)***		(.01)***		(.00)***	
Intimidation						
Victim race/	.55 (.00)	.54 –.56.95–1.00	.65 (.01)***	.62 –.67.95–1.09	.53 (.01)	.49 –.52.09 –.99
ethnicity	***.98	1.16–1.30	1.01 (.03)	1.11 –.148	***.97	1.14–1.29
Black	(.01)		1.28 (.10)		(.02)*	
Hispanic	1.23 (.03)		***		1.21 (.04)	
Other	***				***	
Victim male	1.26 (.01) ***	1.24–1.29	–	–	–	–
Location	1.08 (.01) ***	1.06–1.10	1.12 (.03) ***	1.07–1.17	1.07 (.01) ***	1.05–1.10
Victim age	1.00 (.00) ***	1.00–1.01	1.00 (.00)	.99–1.00	1.01 (.00) ***	1.00–1.01
Injuries to victim	2.11 (.02)	2.08–2.15	2.56 (.05)	2.46–2.66	2.02 (.02)	1.98–2.06
'Minor' injury	***	1.82–2.02	***	2.08–2.61	***	1.72–1.92
'Major' injury	1.92 (.05)		2.33 (.13)		1.82 (.05)	
	***		***		***	
Constant	.59 (.01)***	.57 –.62	.73 (.03)***	.64 –.76	.61 (.01)***	.58 –.63
Pseudo R^2	.06		.08		.06	

Notes: *$p \leq .05$, **$p \leq .01$, ***$p \leq .001$.

Arrest rates for IPV

Table 3 provides a comprehensive report of arrest rates for IPV by arrest policy, offense type, victim race/ethnicity, victim sex, location of the incident, and injuries to the victim as recorded by the responding officer(s). There are relatively few statistically significant differences in arrest rates for IPV between offenders in same-sex and opposite-sex couples and offenders in female and male same-sex couples, and the effect sizes range from minimal to approaching small. All the comparisons included in this section reached statistical significance.

Same-sex couples are more likely to be arrested under mandatory arrest laws (56%) than are opposite-sex couples (55%). Only 21% of acts of intimidation in incidents involving same-sex couples resulted in arrest, fewer than the 28% observed for intimidation in opposite-sex couples. Incidents with white victims in same-sex relationships are less likely to result in arrest (56%) than opposite-sex couples (59%), and incidents with Black victims in same-sex relationships are more likely to result in an arrest (44%) than incidents with Black victims in opposite-sex couples (41%). Incidents with male victims in same-sex relationships are less likely to result in arrest (54%) than are incidents with male victims in opposite-sex couples (57%); however, the arrest rates for incidents with male victims for both groups are still significantly higher than the arrest rates for incidents with female victims (50% and 51%). Finally, arrests are less likely in incidents where the officers observed 'no injuries' among same-sex couples (37%) than opposite-sex couples (39%), but arrests were more likely in incidents with observed injuries for both same-sex and opposite-sex couples.

When comparing arrest rates for female same-sex couples and male same-sex couples, only three statistically significant differences emerged. First, arrest rates for aggravated assault are lower for female same-sex couples (55%) than male same-sex couples (61%). Incidents that took place in the victim's residence are also less likely to result in arrest for female same-sex couples (52%) than incidents among male same-sex couples (55%). Finally, incidents where 'minor' injuries were observed are less likely to result in arrest for female same-sex couples (61%) than for incidents involving male same-sex couples (53%).

Replication of **Pattavina et al. (2007)**

In Tables 4 and 5, we replicate Pattavina et al.'s 2007 analysis with 2016 NIBRS data. Most of the results are consistent with their analysis; however, they found that mandatory arrest policies did not increase the likelihood of arrest for male same-sex couples (see Table 4). Instead, we find that mandatory arrest policies significantly increase the likelihood of arrest for IPV for all same-sex couples (OR = 1.28), as well as male (OR = 1.34) and female (OR = 1.25) same-sex couples after controlling for offense types, victim race/ethnicity and sex, and the location of the incident.

Furthermore, aggravated assaults in 2016 are no more likely than simple assaults to result in arrest for all same-sex and female same-sex couples. This is a change from the 2000 data, where aggravated assaults were significantly more likely than simple assaults to end in an arrest for all same-sex couples and male same-sex couples. In our analysis, aggravated assaults in male same-sex couples are 1.26 times more likely to result in arrest ($p \leq .05$) than simple assaults, which is consistent with the results from the 2000 data. Incidents involving intimidation were .21 times less likely to result in arrest for all same-sex couples ($p \leq .001$) and female same-sex couples ($p \leq .001$), and .20 times less likely to result in arrest for male same-sex couples ($p \leq .001$), than were simple assaults.

The pattern of results of arrest based on victim race and sex is the same for the 2000 and 2016 data. For all same-sex and female same-sex couples, incidents involving nonwhite victims are .61 times less likely to result in an arrest ($p \leq .001$) than incidents involving white victims. Incidents with nonwhite victims in male same-sex couples are .62 times less likely to result in an arrest ($p \leq .001$) than incidents with white victims. There was no relationship between observed victim sex and arrest for all the same-sex and all the opposite-sex couples.

When comparing the results of the models for all opposite-sex incidents, opposite-sex incidents involving a female victim, and opposite-sex incidents with a male victim, all of the independent variables achieve statistical significance (see Table 5). This is consistent with Pattavina et al. (2007) and is likely due to the large sample size. For every opposite-sex relationship type, incidents that fall under mandatory arrest statutes are significantly more likely to result in arrest than incidents that occur in jurisdictions with pro- or discretionary arrest statutes. For opposite-sex couples as a whole, aggravated assaults are significantly more likely (OR = 1.27), and acts of intimidation are significantly less likely (OR = .31), to result in arrest than incidents of simple assault. Incidents involving nonwhite victims are significantly less likely (OR = .63) to result in arrest as compared to white victims, incidents involving male victims are significantly more likely (OR = 1.27) to result in arrest than those with female victims, and incidents occurring at the victim's residence are significantly more likely (OR = 1.09) to result in arrest than those occurring elsewhere. These same patterns hold true for opposite-sex incidents with male victims and opposite-sex incidents with female victims. All of the directions of these effects are identical to those reported in the Pattavina et al. (2007) analysis.

Expanding the 2007 model

However, when we extend the model for all, female, and male same-sex couples by adding additional variables to indicate whether the arrest policy was mandatory, pro-, or discretionary arrest, whether the victim was white, Black, Hispanic, or of another racial group, and whether the officer observed 'no injury,' 'minor injury,' or 'major injury' to the victim, important differences emerge. As shown in Table 6, by using the additional categories for victim race and ethnicity, we see that the negative association between being a nonwhite victim and a decreased likelihood of arrest of the offender is actually attributable to the effect of the victim being Black. For all, female, and male same-sex couples, incidents involving Black victims are only .60, .59, and .60 times as likely to result in arrest than incidents with white victims ($p \leq .001$). Incidents involving Hispanic victims or victims of another racial group are no more or less likely to result in an arrest than white victims.

Furthermore, when the additional independent variables are added to the model, the relationship between mandatory arrest policies and arrest for IPV among male same-sex couples is no longer significant. When a male offender commits violence against a male intimate partner, the likelihood of arrest does not change whether the incident is committed in a mandatory, pro-, or discretionary arrest state. This is a departure from Pattavina et al. (2007), who found that incidents among male same-sex couples in mandatory arrest states were more likely to result in arrest than incidents in states without mandatory arrest policies.

Additionally, incidents among all, female, and male same-sex couples in pro-arrest states are no more or less likely to result in arrest than those in discretionary arrest states. This lack of an effect of pro-arrest policies is not consistent with Durfee and Fetzer (2014), who analyzed 2010 NIBRS data and found that incidents among opposite-sex couples occurring in pro-arrest states were more likely to result in arrest than those in discretionary arrest states (same-sex couples were not included in the analysis). It is also inconsistent with the results presented in Table 7 for all opposite-sex couples (whether a male or female victim), which indicates that among opposite-sex couples, incidents in pro-arrest states are 1.05 times more likely to result in an arrest than incidents in discretionary arrest states ($p \leq .001$ for all opposite sex and opposite sex/male victims; $p \leq .01$ for opposite sex/female victims). Simply put, there is no evidence that for incidents between same-sex couples in the 2016 NIBRS, officers are more likely to make an arrest when the preferred (but not mandatory) outcome – according to state statute – is to make an arrest.

Finally, as shown in Table 6, the injuries observed by the officer are significantly related to the likelihood of arrest for all, female, and male same-sex couples. When the officer observes a 'minor injury' (as compared to 'no injury'), they are 2.27 times more likely to make an arrest for all same-sex couples, 2.10 times more likely in cases with female same-sex couples, and 2.62 times more likely for male same-sex couples ($p \leq .001$). Similarly, observing 'major injury' (as compared to 'no injury') increases the likelihood of arrest 2.29 times for all same-sex couples, 1.97 times for female same-sex couples, and 2.80 times for male same-sex couples ($p \leq .001$). Victim age was only statistically significant for incidents involving male same-sex couples (OR = 1.01); as victim age increases, the likelihood of the officer arresting the offender also increases.

As for the extended model with the opposite-sex couples (Table 7), only one change was observed from the model presented in Table 4. For all opposite-sex couple types, incidents involving Black victims are significantly less likely (OR = .55 for all, .65 for male victims, and .53 for female victims), and incidents involving victims of another race are significantly more likely (OR = 1.23 for all, 1.28 for male victims, and 1.21 for female victims) to result in the arrest of the offender than incidents with white victims. Similarly, for all opposite-sex couples with female victims (OR = .97), incidents with Hispanic victims are significantly less likely to result in arrest than incidents with white victims. However, for all opposite-sex incidents, and opposite-sex incidents with male victims, incidents with Hispanic victims are no more or less likely than incidents with white victims to result in arrest.

Given the patterns of results presented here, we created an interaction term to capture the additional effect of the victim being both Black and female on the likelihood of arrest and ran a replication of all models presented here. None of those models showed any difference in the statistical significance of the independent variables, nor was the direction of the effects changed, so we omitted the interaction term from the extended models.

Discussion

This paper replicates and extends Pattavina et al.'s (2007) analysis of arrests for IPV among same-sex, opposite-sex, same-sex female, and same-sex male couples. Both Pattavina et al. and our analysis use the NIBRS, which contains all cases of IPV reported to law enforcement in the United States. Our analysis uses 2016 data from 39 states, while theirs uses 2000 data from 19 states. It is notable that a larger proportion of IPV incidents reported to police involve same-sex couples (2.2% vs. 0.6%), potentially indicating a greater willingness of same-sex IPV victims to contact police during or after a violent incident. Otherwise, the pattern of our results is strikingly similar to those of Pattavina et al. We find nearly identical arrest rates in 2016 (between 52% and 54%) as they did with 2000 data. However, using their model, we find that offenders in male same-sex couples are significantly more likely to be arrested under mandatory arrest policies as compared to pro- or discretionary arrest policies, while they found no difference between these policies. Additionally, for all and female same-sex couples, offenders who commit aggravated assaults are no more likely than offenders committing simple assaults to be arrested.

Extending their model to include additional types of victim race/ethnicity led to the discovery that for same-sex couples, the decreased likelihood of arrest when the victim was nonwhite as compared to white did not hold true when the victim was Hispanic or of another race. Among same-sex couples, only incidents with Black victims were significantly less likely to result in arrest than incidents with white victims. In addition, refining the model to differentiate between mandatory arrest, pro-arrest policies, and discretionary arrest policies resulted in changes to the impacts of mandatory arrest policies. For incidents involving male same-sex couples, neither mandatory nor pro-arrest policies were associated with the probability of arrest as compared to those incidents in discretionary states.

Some of these results are fairly unsurprising. It makes sense that in general, arrest is more likely in jurisdictions that require arrest; that data is consistent with previous studies of mandatory arrest laws. It also makes sense that arrest rates are higher when police classify cases as aggravated assault; more serious offenses generally prompt greater police intervention. The greater number of female victims in opposite-sex couples is also consistent with years of research on gender and victimization, notwithstanding the contentions of some scholars that men and women are equally violent in relationships (Johnson, 2006; Kimmel, 2002) and that men are prevented by concerns about perceptions of masculinity from coming forward with their experiences of victimization (Durfee, 2011). The higher rates of aggravated assaults in male same-sex relationships are consistent with research suggesting that men committing acts of IPV tend to use greater force and cause more injury than women (Capaldi et al., 2009).

It also makes sense that officers would be more likely to make an arrest when victims have visible 'minor' and 'major' injuries than in cases where no injury is observed. The presence and severity of victim injuries are associated with both arrest and prosecution of offenders for IPV (Buel & Hirst, 2009; Deutsch et al., 2017). Victim injuries are those that are observed by the officer. Some officers, however, do not ask about or take photos of injuries (Deutsch et al., 2017). Moreover, some injuries are not apparent, or appear less serious, at the time of the incident. Recent developments in technology may render some injuries more visible. For example, while 93% of the 172 strangulation victims examined in one study had no apparent injury, when alternate light source (ALS) technology was used, injuries were observed on 98% of the victims (Holbrook & Jackson, 2013). The visibility of injuries may also be a factor as to why incidents with Black victims are less likely to result in arrest than those with white victims. Many injuries are more apparent on lighter skin and less apparent on darker skin (Baker & Sommers, 2008; Deutsch et al., 2017), making incidents involving Black victims appear to be less serious than those with white victims.

Scholars have long contended that stereotypes about victims and offenders in cases of IPV – both in opposite-sex and same-sex relationships – influence how those individuals are treated by the legal system. Goodmark (2008) has argued that the 'paradigmatic victim' of IPV is passive, white, and heterosexual, and that victims with those traits are more likely to receive assistance from the legal system. Our data is consistent with those arguments. Although injuries are more likely in same-sex relationships, arrest rates are the same for same-sex and opposite-sex relationships, which suggests that police are not intervening as decisively in cases involving same-sex relationships. Offenders in female same-sex relationships, for example, may be less likely to be arrested than their male counterparts overall and less likely to be arrested for incidents resulting in minor injuries because violence between women is seen as less serious or because men are thought to present a greater threat to their partners – male or female – than women are (Goodmark, 2008). This interpretation is consistent with Pattavina et al. (2007), who argued that societal stereotypes about women influenced their rates of arrest, especially in states without mandatory arrest laws. Furthermore, Pattavina et al. found that the incorporation of 'inclusive language' in legal statutes significantly increased the likelihood of arrest in incidents with male same-sex couples. Although changes in the legal landscape have extended protection to individuals in same-sex relationships, and there is a greater acceptance of same-sex couples since Pattavina et al. conducted their research, our research is consistent with their understanding of why male same-sex couples might have higher rates of arrest than female same-sex couples.

The lower rates of arrest for intimidation and in cases with no injuries in same-sex relationships may also reflect these stereotypes. Police may be less concerned about the seriousness of a threat or the likelihood of further injury when made by a same-sex partner than when made by a man against a woman (Goodmark, 2008, 2012). Similarly, although victims in same-sex relationships are more likely to be Black, arrests are less likely in incidents involving Black victims. This disparity may reflect the continued operation of victim stereotypes about race (Goodmark, 2008, 2012), despite the fact that police in mandatory arrest jurisdictions are now making arrests at essentially the same rates in same-sex and opposite-sex relationships. Finally, at the bivariate level, arrest rates in incidents involving male victims are higher in both opposite-sex (57%) and same-sex relationships (54%) than in incidents with female victims (51% and 50%, respectively), and in the logistic regression models, this association still holds true for opposite-sex couples. This could reflect the greater attention that has been paid in recent years to the needs of male victims of IPV, but could also indicate the higher standards to which police hold female victims, requiring them to conform to victim stereotypes involving passivity, whiteness, and heterosexuality to warrant intervention (Goodmark, 2008, 2012). While attitudes towards same-sex relationships may be changing, entrenched stereotypes around IPV may nonetheless make it more difficult for some individuals in same-sex relationships to get protection from the law. Additional research about the impacts of victim sex on the arrest decision in same-sex relationships is needed. Such research might compare police perceptions of injury inflicted by and culpability of men and women accused of committing IPV in heterosexual and same-sex relationships.

There are, of course, limitations in our data. First, this data comes from the 2016 NIBRS, and although it represents the first year of data collection after Obergefell v. Hodges, many jurisdictions may not have had time to fully implement and train officers as to the changes in mandatory arrest policies as applied to same-sex couples. Additionally, NIBRS data are reported by law enforcement and compiled by the FBI. The data contain only the victim sex, race, and ethnicity reported by the officer, which may not reflect the actual social identities of the victim and the offender. In addition, victim sex is defined as 'male' or 'female' and is biologically (and likely legally) based, which is a serious limitation when analyzing intimate relationships.

Even our ability to characterize these relationships is hampered by the codes used by the FBI for the relationship between the victim and the offender. The term 'homosexual relationship' is outdated, clinical, offensive, and does not allow researchers to examine the complexities of relationship type on arrest for IPV in the same ways that we can for individuals in opposite-sex relationships (who are classified as spouses, ex-spouses, common-law spouses, boyfriend/girlfriend, etc.). We encourage the FBI to consider removing the 'homosexual relationship' category from the NIBRS to more accurately reflect the legal status of same-sex couples in the United States. This has been done in the past – in 2012, the FBI removed the word 'forcible' from the definition of rape and defined rape in gender neutral terms, which allowed for more accurate reporting of rapes and for the inclusion of male rapes for the first time in FBI databases in 2013 (FBI, 2013). While we believe a wider conversation is needed before a replacement term(s) is suggested, from a data analysis perspective, it would make more sense to remove the 'homosexual relationship' category altogether and then modify 'boyfriend/girlfriend' to 'romantic or dating partners.' By doing so, police would be forced to report more accurate and more comparable relationship data for everyone, and it would increase our ability to conduct more sophisticated analyses about same-sex and opposite-sex IPV.

Furthermore, our small sample size limits our ability to conduct a more nuanced analysis of the effect that victim race and ethnicity has on the likelihood of arrest. Given the few incidents of IPV with Native Americans, Asians, and Pacific Islanders and Native Hawaiians victims who are in same-sex partnerships in the 2016 NIBRS (there are only 19 Native American, 16 Asian, and 2 Native Hawaiian or other Pacific Islanders incidents with male victims in same-sex partnerships), it is impossible to include these as categories in the logistic regression models. Future research should aggregate years of the NIBRS post-2015 (when same-sex marriage became legal in the United States) in order to analyze the arrest decision in incidents with these victims.

Because of the limitations of the data, we do not know the sexual orientations of the victim and offender, so we cannot characterize relationships beyond 'same sex' and 'opposite sex.' Our results should not be interpreted as anything more than female same-sex and male same-sex victims – we do not know if they are involved in gay, lesbian, or other types of relationships. Our results also do not speak to the experiences of all of those within the lesbian, gay, bisexual, transgender, queer, intersex, and asexual (LGBTQIA) community, most notably bisexual, transgender, and gender fluid individuals. We note, however, that rates of IPV are high in those communities, and that transgender and bisexual women particularly are at elevated risk of victimization (Walters, Chen, & Breidig, 2013).

Given the often-problematic nature of the relationship between the police, the courts, and the LGBTQIA community – especially for those LGBTQIA individuals of color – the fact that mandatory arrest policies are having a greater impact on same-sex couples than they did in 2000 should give us pause. Nearly equivalent arrest rates for opposite- and same-sex couples will not be universally seen as good news, particularly given the historic wariness with which LGBTQIA individuals have approached police intervention. Police intervention is not a proxy for equality in access to legal protections and other resources for LGBTQIA survivors. Moreover, concerns about the criminalization of IPV and its relationship to mass incarceration are growing among scholars and anti-violence advocates (Goodmark, 2018). Mandatory arrest policies are part of the apparatus of criminalization; seeing them applied more broadly may be concerning for those who believe that such policies do more harm than good.

Disclosure statement

No potential conflict of interest was reported by the authors.

References

Alhusen, J.L., Lucea, M.B., & Glass, N. (2010). Perceptions of and experience with system responses to female same sex intimate partner violence. *Partner Abuse, 1*, 443–462.

Baker, N.L., Buick, J.D., Kim, S.R., Moniz, S., & Nava, K.L. (2013). Lessons from examining same-sex intimate partner violence. *Sex Roles, 69*(3–4), 182–192.

Baker, R.B., & Sommers, M.S. (2008). Physical injury from intimate partner violence: Measurement strategies and challenges. *Journal of Obstetric, Gynecologic & Neonatal Nursing, 37*(2), 228–233.

Berk, R.A., Campbell, A., Klap, R., & Western, B. (1992). Bayesian analysis of the Colorado Springs spouse abuse experiment. *Journal of Criminal Law and Criminology, 83*(1), 170–200.

Branch, K.A., Khan, S., & Dretsch, E. (2018). Same sex intimate partner violence. In C.M. Hilinski-Rosick & D.R. Lee (Eds.), *Contemporary issues in victimology: Identifying patterns and trends* (pp. 115–130). Lanham, MD: Lexington Books.

Brown, T.N.T., & Herman, J.L. (2015). *Intimate partner violence and sexual abuse among LGBT people: A review of existing research*. Los Angeles, CA: Williams Institute.

Buel, S.M., & Hirst, E.M. (2009). Medical and forensic documentation. In C. Mitchell & D. Anglin (Eds.), *Intimate partner violence: A health-based perspective* (pp. 443–458). New York: Oxford University Press.

Bunker Rohrbaug, J. (2006). Domestic violence in same-gender relationships. *Family Court Review, 44* (2), 287–299.

Burke, T.W., Jordan, M.L., & Owen, S.S. (2002). A cross-national comparison of gay and lesbian domestic violence. *Journal of Contemporary Criminal Justice, 18*(3), 231–257.

Busch, A.L., & Rosenberg, M.S. (2004). Comparing women and men arrested for domestic violence: A preliminary report. *Journal of Family Violence, 19*(1), 49–57.

Capaldi, D.M., Shortt, J.W., Kim, H.K., Wilson, J., Crosby, L., & Tucci, S. (2009). Official incidents of domestic violence: Types, injury, and associations with nonofficial couple aggression. *Violence and Victims, 24*(4), 502–519.

Chesney-Lind, M. (2002). Criminalizing victimization: The unintended consequences of pro-arrest policies for girls and women. *Criminology & Public Policy, 82*, 81–90.

Colvin, R.A. (2012). *Gay and lesbian cops: Diversity and effective policing*. Boulder, CO: Lynne Rienner Publishers.

Connecticut Coalition Against Domestic Violence. (2018). *Dominant aggressor: Reducing decades of dual arrest in Connecticut*. Retrieved from http://www.ctcadv.org/files/7215/1922/7366/DominantAggressor2.18.pdf

DeLeon-Granados, W., Wells, W., & Binsbacher, R. (2006). Arresting developments: Trends in female arrests for domestic violence and proposed explanations. *Violence against Women, 12*(4), 355–371.

Deutsch, L.S., Resch, K., Barber, T., Zuckerman, Y., Stone, J.T., & Cerulli, C. (2017). Bruise documentation, race and barriers to seeking legal relief for intimate partner violence survivors: A retrospective qualitative study. *Journal of Family Violence, 32*(8), 767–773.

Dugan, L. (2003). Domestic violence legislation: Exploring its impact on the likelihood of domestic violence, police involvement, and arrest. *National Consortium on Violence Research, 2*, 283–312.

Dunford, F.W., Huizinga, D., & Elliott, D.S. (1990). The role of arrest in domestic assault: the Omaha police experiment. *Criminology, 28*(2), 183–206.

Durfee, A. (2011). "I'm not a victim, she's an abuser": Masculinity, victimization, and protective orders. *Gender and Society, 25*(3), 316–334.

Durfee, A. (2012). Situational ambiguity and gendered patterns of arrest for intimate partner violence. *Violence against Women, 18*(1), 64–84.

Durfee, A., & Fetzer, M.D. (2014). Offense type and the arrest decision in cases of intimate partner violence. *Crime and Delinquency, 62*(7), 954–977.

Federal Bureau of Investigation. (2013). *Crime in the United States, 2013*. Retrieved from https://ucr.fbi.gov/crime-in-the-u.s/2013/crime-in-the-u.s.-2013/violent-crime/rape

Federal Bureau of Investigation (2017). *Data declaration: Number of agencies and population covered by population group, 2016*. Retrieved from https://ucr.fbi.gov/nibrs/2016/tables/data-declarations/dd_number_of_agencies_and_population_covered_by_population_group_2016_final.pdf.

Federal Bureau of Investigation. (n.d.). *National Incident-Based Reporting System (NIBRS)*. Retrieved from https://www.fbi.gov/services/cjis/ucr/nibrs.

Finneran, C., & Stephenson, R. (2013). Gay and bisexual men's perception of police helpfulness in response to male-male intimate partner violence. *Western Journal of Emergency Medicine: Integrating Emergency Care with Population Health, 14*(4), 354–362.

Franklin, C.A., Goodson, A., & Garza, A.D. (2019). Intimate partner violence among sexual minorities: Predicting police officer arrest decisions. *Criminal Justice and Behavior, xx*, 1–19.

Frye, V., Haviland, M., & Rajah, V. (2007). Dual arrest and other unintended consequences of mandatory arrest in New York City: A brief report. *Journal of Family Violence, 22*(6), 397–405.

Garner, J.H., Fagan, J.A., & Maxwell, C.D. (1995). Published findings from the spouse assault replication program: A critical review. *Journal of Quantitative Criminology, 11*, 3–28.

Gee, P.W. (1983). Ensuring police protection for battered women: The Scott v. Hart Suit. *Signs, 8*, 554–567.

Girshick, L. B. (2002). No sugar, no spice: Reflections on research on woman-to-woman sexual violence. *Violence against Women, 8*(12), 1500–1520.

GLAAD (n.d.). *Glossary of Terms - Lesbian/Gay/Bisexual/Queer*. Retrieved from https://www.glaad.org/reference/lgbtq

Goodmark, L. (2008). When is a battered woman not a battered woman? When she fights back. *Yale Journal of Law and Feminism, 20*, 76–129.

Goodmark, L. (2012). *A troubled marriage: Domestic violence and the legal system*. New York: NYU Press.

Goodmark, L. (2013). Transgender people, intimate partner abuse, and the legal system. *Harvard Civil Rights-civil Liberties Law Review, 48*, 51–104.

Goodmark, L. (2018). *Decriminalizing domestic violence: A balanced policy approach to intimate partner violence*. Oakland: University of California Press.

Goodmark, L. (2020). Transgender intimate partner violence and legal system reform. In A. Messinger & X. Guadalupe-Diaz (Eds.), *Transgender intimate partner violence: A comprehensive introduction*. New York: NYU Press.

Hafemeister, T.L. (2011). If all you have is a hammer: Society's ineffective response to intimate partner violence. *Catholic University Law Review, 60*, 919–1001.

Hassouneh, D., & Glass, N. (2008). The influence of gender role stereotyping on women's experiences of female same sex intimate partner violence. *Violence against Women, 14*(3), 310–325.

Hirschel, D., & Buzawa, E. (2002). Understanding the context of dual arrest with directions for future research. *Violence against Women, 8*(12), 1449–1473.

Hirschel, D., Buzawa, E., Pattavina, A., & Faggiani, D. (2007). Domestic violence and mandatory arrest laws: To what extent do they influence police arrest decisions? *Journal of Criminal Law and Criminology, 98*, 255–298.

Hirschel, D., Buzawa, E., Pattavina, A., Faggiani, D., & Reuland, M. (2007). *Explaining the prevalence, context, and consequences of dual arrest in intimate partner cases*. Retrieved from https://www.ncjrs.gov/pdffiles1/nij/grants/218355.pdf.

Hirschel, D., & Deveau, L. (2017). The impact of primary aggressor laws on single versus dual arrest in incidents of intimate partner violence. *Violence against Women, 23*(10), 1155–1176.

Hirschel, J.D., Hutchison, I., & Dean, C.W. (1992). The failure of arrest to deter spouse abuse. *Journal of Research in Crime and Delinquency, 29*(1), 7–33.

Holbrook, D.S., & Jackson, M.C. (2013). Use of an alternative Light Source to Assess Strangulation Victims. *Journal of Forensic Nursing, 9*(3), 140–145.

Houston, C. (2014). How feminist theory became (criminal) law: Tracing the path to mandatory criminal intervention in domestic violence cases. *Michigan Journal of Gender and the Law, 21*, 217–272.

Hunter, N.D. (2000). Sexuality and civil rights: Re-imagining anti-discrimination laws. *New York Law School Journal of Human Rights, 17*, 565–587.

Iowa Code Ann. §§ 236.12 (2)(a)).

Iyengar, R. (2009). Does the certainty of arrest reduce domestic violence? Evidence from mandatory and recommended arrest laws. *Journal of Public Economics, 93*(1–2), 85–98.

Johnson, M.P. (2006). Conflict and control: Gender symmetry and asymmetry in domestic violence. *Violence against Women, 12*(11), 1003–1018.

Kimmel, M.S. (2002). "Gender symmetry" in domestic violence: A substantive and methodological research review. *Violence against Women, 8*(11), 1332–1363.

Kuehnle, K., & Sullivan, A. (2003). Gay and lesbian victimization: Reporting factors in domestic violence and bias incidents. *Criminal Justice and Behavior, 30*(1), 85–96.

Lakens, D. (2013). *Calculating and reporting effect sizes to facilitate cumulative science: a practical primer for t-tests and ANOVAs*. Retrieved from https://www.frontiersin.org/articles/10.3389/fpsyg.2013.00863/full

Letellier, P. (1994). Gay and bisexual male domestic violence victimization: Challenges to feminist theory and responses to violence. *Violence and Victims, 9*(2), 95–106.

Maxwell, C.D., Garner, J.H., & Fagan, J.A. (2002). The preventive effects of arrest on intimate partner violence: Research, policy and theory. *Criminology Public Policy, 2*(1), 51–80.

Messing, J.T., Campbell, J., Wilson, J.S., Brown, S., Patchell, B., & Shall, C. (2014). *Police departments' use of the Lethality Assessment Program: A quasi-experimental evaluation*. Retrieved from https://www.ncjrs.gov/pdffiles1/nij/grants/247456.pdf.

Messinger, A.M. (2017). *LGBTQ intimate partner violence: Lessons for policy, practice, and research*. Oakland, CA: University of California Press.

Miles-Johnson, T. (2013). Confidence and trust in police: How sexual identity difference shapes perceptions of police. *Current Issues in Criminal Justice, 25*(2), 685–702.

Miller, S.L., & Meloy, M.L. (2006). Women's use of force: Voices of women arrested for domestic violence. *Violence against Women, 12*(1), 89–115.

Morrison, A.M. (2003). Queering domestic violence to "straighten out" criminal law: What might happen when queer theory and practice meet criminal law's conventional responses to domestic violence. *Southern California Review of Law and Women's Studies, 13*, 81–160.

Nadal, K.L., Quintanilla, A., Goswick, A., & Sriken, J. (2015). Lesbian, gay, bisexual, and queer people's perceptions of the criminal justice system: implications for social services. *Journal of Gay & Lesbian Social Services, 27*(4), 457–481.

National Archive of Criminal Justice Data. *National incident-based reporting system, 2000: Extract files*. (2009, September 14). Ann Arbor, MI: Inter-university Consortium for Political and Social Research [distributor].

National Archive of Criminal Justice Data. (2018, August 17). *National incident-based reporting system, 2016: Extract files*. Ann Arbor, MI: Inter-university Consortium for Political and Social Research [distributor].

National Coalition of Anti-Violence Programs. (2018). *Lesbian, gay, bisexual, transgender, queer and HIV-affected hate and intimate partner violence in 2017*. New York, NY: Author.

Novisky, M.A., & Peralta, R.L. (2015). When women tell: Intimate partner violence and the factors related to police notification. *Violence against Women, 21*(1), 65–86.

Obergefell v. Hodges. (2015). 135 S.Ct. 2071.

Owen, S.S., Burke, T.W., Few-Demo, A.L., & Natwick, J. (2018). Perceptions of the police by LGBT communities. *American Journal of Criminal Justice, 43*(3), 668–693.

Parry, M.M., & O'Neal, E.N. (2015). Help-seeking behavior among same sex intimate partner violence victims: An intersectional argument. *Criminology, Criminal Justice Law & Society, 16*, 51–67.

Pate, A.M., & Hamilton, E.E. (1992). Formal and informal deterrents to domestic violence: The Dade County spouse assault experiment. *American Sociological Review, 57*(5), 691–697.

Pattavina, A., Hirschel, D., Buzawa, E., Faggiani, D., & Bentley, H. (2007). A comparison of the Police Response to Heterosexual Versus Same-Sex Intimate Partner Violence. *Violence against Women, 13*(4), 374–394.

Pew Research Center. (2019). Attitudes on same sex marriage. Retrieved from https://www.pewforum.org/fact-sheet/changing-attitudes-on-gay-marriage/

R.I. Gen. Laws § 12-29-3 (b), (c).

Renzetti, C.M. (1997). Violence in lesbian and gay relationships. In L.L. O'Toole & J.R. Schiffman (Eds.), *Gender Violence: Interdisciplinary perspectives* (pp. 285–293). New York: New York University Press.

Richards, T.N., Tudor, A., & Gover, A.R. (2018). An updated assessment of personal protective order statutes in the United States: have statutes become more progressive in the past decade? *Violence against Women, 24*(7), 816–842.

Ristock, J.L. (2002). *No more secrets: Violence in lesbian relationships*. New York, NY: Routledge.

Roe & Jagodinsky. (n.d.). Power and control wheel for lesbian, gay, bisexual, and trans relationships. National Domestic Violence Hotline. Retrieved from http://www.thehotline.org/wp-content/uploads/sites/3/2015/01/LGBT-Wheel.pdf.

Rollè, L., Giardina, G., Caldarera, A.M., Gerino, E., & Brustia, P. (2018). When intimate partner violence meets same sex couples: A review of same sex intimate partner violence. *Frontiers in Psychology, 9*, 1506.

Sherman, L.W., & Berk, R.A. (1984). The specific deterrent effects of arrest for domestic assault. *American Sociological Review, 49*(2), 261–272.

Sherman, L.W., & Harris, H.M. (2015). Increased death rates of domestic violence victims from arresting vs. warning suspects in the Milwaukee Domestic Violence Experiment (MilDVE). *Journal of Experimental Criminology, 11*(1), 1–20.

Sugarman, D.B., & Boney-McCoy, S. (2000). Research synthesis in family violence: The art of reviewing the research. *Journal of Aggression, Maltreatment & Trauma, 4*(1), 55–82.

Swan, S., & Snow, D. (2002). A typology of women's use of violence in intimate relationships. *Violence against Women, 8*(3), 286–319.

Thurman v. City of Torrington. (1984). 595 F. Supp. 1521 (D. Conn.)

Walters, M.L., Chen, J., & Breidig, M.J. (2013). *The national intimate partner and sexual violence survey (NISVS): 2010 findings on victimization by sexual orientation*. Atlanta, GA: National Center for Injury Prevention and Control, Centers for Disease Control and Prevention.

Wolf, M.E., Ly, U., Hobart, M.A., & Kernic, M.A. (2003). Barriers to seeking police help for intimate partner violence. *Journal of Family Violence, 18*(2), 121–129.

Barriers stopping LGBTI people from accessing LGBTI police liaison officers: analysing interviews with community and police

Angela Dwyer, Matthew Ball, Murray Lee, Thomas Crofts and Christine Bond

ABSTRACT
Police liaison programs that support LGBTI (lesbian, gay, bisexual, transgender, intersex) people might go by many names (including GLLOs, LGBTI police liaison officers, etc.), but they have become the key model for providing police service enhancements for LGBTI people. These programs now dominate approaches used by police to build relationships between police and LGBTI communities, yet research on the effectiveness of these programs is limited. This paper examines interview data from LGBTI people and LGBTI police liaison officers in three states in Australia. The interviews were part of a broader study of LGBTI police liaison programs, which included a survey of LGBTI people about the issues they think impact upon these programs. The analysis demonstrates the key issues that stop LGBTI people from seeking support from LGBTI police liaison officers and how we might potentially improve this situation.

Historically, relationships between police and lesbian, gay, bisexual, transgender, and intersex (LGBTI) people have been problematic due to the criminalisation of sodomy (Fradella & Grundy, 2016; see also American Civil Liberties Union, 2017) and discriminatory policing practices (Colvin, 2012a; Dwyer, 2014; Lambda Legal, 2015; Mallory, Hasenbush, & Sears, 2015). The policing of these communities has been traditionally informed by the notion that sexuality-, gender-, or sex-diversity was immoral and in need of regulation and criminalisation (Groombridge, 1999). Police organisations have also dedicated time and resources to building relationships with LGBTI people (Tomsen, 2009), including activities like community consultation committees and appearances at major LGBTI events (like marching in uniform in the Sydney Gay and Lesbian Mardi Gras). With the broad focus of police organisations on policing vulnerable people (Bartkowiak-Theron & Asquith, 2012), LGBTI-police relations have improved when compared to the overtly discriminatory policing practices of the past (Dario, Fradella, Verhagen, & Parry, 2020; Owen, Burke, Few-Demo, & Natwick, 2017; Tomsen, 2009), but these relationships are still tenuous (Russell, 2020).

LGBTI police liaison officer programs are a key service enhancement strategy by police organisations adopted to build relationships with LGBTI people and to support LGBTI victims. They were established around Australia from the late 1980s onwards to ameliorate historically problematic LGBTI-police relations. Many police organisations around Australia (Dwyer & Ball, 2013) and internationally (Colvin, 2012b; Copple & Dunn, 2017; Out to Protect, 2016) now have dedicated liaison programs that comprise typically volunteer police officers trained about LGBTI issues and do this role in addition to other duties associated with their substantive role as an officer. Liaison officers are trained to understand LGBTI issues and are typically available to support LGBTI people in circumstances where they have been a victim, an offender, or even a witness to a crime. The officers are usually available when a LGBTI person wants to speak to them, providing a key form of frontline support for LGBTI people. Interestingly, though, research indicates that while many LGBTI people are aware of these liaison officers, very few actually access them, and they do so infrequently (Berman & Robinson, 2010). This is even more paradoxical given that research highlights how people using these services feel better supported than those accessing mainstream police (Leonard, Mitchell, Patel, & Fox, 2008).

This article examines the results of a project exploring LGBTI police liaison services across three states in Australia (Queensland, New South Wales, and Western Australia) to investigate the gap between awareness and access of these services. As part of a mixed-methods study, interviews were then conducted with LGBTI people to explore in-depth their experiences with LGBTI police liaison officers and the reasons they did or did not report victimisation to these officers. This paper focuses on the results of the qualitative interviews conducted for the project to answer a key question: what stops LGBTI people seeking support from LGBTI police liaison officers? We first discuss existing research literature in this area, followed by outlining the methodology we employed. We then examine the key themes that emerged from the analysis of the interviews. Finally, we present the key implications of our findings for policy and practice development in police and LGBTI community services.

Why examine LGBTI police liaison programs now?

Police organisations do invest money and police time to build relationships with diverse, marginalised communities in different ways, but these can be difficult to sustain in police organisations with limited resources (Skilling, 2016). It is therefore important that we not take these forms of relationship building for granted and attempt to understand the kinds of work they are doing and the relationships they are making possible. Two areas of research indicate the need to unpack how LGBTI people engage with police liaison services to better understand the gap between awareness and access of these services, in addition to an apparent lack of research specifically elaborating on LGBTI police liaison services.

LGBTI victimisation is increasing and victims tend not to report

LGBTI communities have been victimised in public, private, and institutional spaces for some time (Hunter, 1990; Peel, 1999). Indeed, research reveals discrimination and abuse (verbal, physical, sexual, psychological, economic) perpetrated against LGBTI people by strangers (Harry, 1990; Mason, 1993), school peers (Hillier et al., 2010), work colleagues (Couch et al., 2007), family (Berrill, 1992), and even justice system actors (Amnesty International, 2005; Mallory et al., 2015; Seabrook, 1992). Research suggests LGBTI people experience nearly twice the level of public violence as their heterosexual counterparts (Herek, Cogan, & Gillis, 2002), with LGBTI people experiencing consistently higher levels of victimisation (Leonard et al., 2008) than the general Australian public. The higher levels of violence are especially concerning given reporting is decreasing among LGBTI adults. For instance, Australian research reports 87% of 600 New South Wales respondents (Attorney Generals Department of NSW, 2003), 75% of 1,094 Queensland respondents (Berman & Robinson, 2010), and 57% of 339 Victorian respondents (Leonard et al., 2008) in LGBTI communities did not report homophobic victimisation to police. LGBTI victims may fear the outcomes of reporting, including police homophobia, disclosure of LGBTI status, rejection from family/friends, and embarrassment about victimisation (Berman & Robinson, 2010; Pattavina, Hirschel, Buzawa, Faggiani, & Bentley, 2007). They may also make assumptions about reporting processes, such as assuming police will minimise incident seriousness, think it is a mutual fight in intimate partner violence, mistreat and further victimise them, fail to protect them, judge them as at fault, assess the incident as too trivial/not reportable, or suggest reporting is futile because the offender will not be located (Pattavina et al., 2007). Similar concerns have been noted abroad (Amnesty International, 2005; Briones-Robinson, Powers, & Socia, 2016; Williams & Robinson, 2004).

Police responses can be unsupportive when LGBTI victimisation is reported

A key reason why LGBTI people do not report victimisation relates to unsupportive and unhelpful police responses. Police-LGBTI interactions have been discriminatory and violent (Dwyer, 2014) and research shows unhelpful police responses including failing to arrest perpetrators, failing to intervene to protect LGBTI people, and not considering an offence a criminal issue unless it is serious (Amnesty International, 2005; Briones-Robinson et al., 2016; Miles-Johnson, 2013a; Pattavina et al., 2007; Wolff & Cokely, 2007). Other research shows how police can assess who the perpetrator is in cases of same-sex intimate partner violence by examining who is 'butch' and 'femme' (and 'noticeable differences in size'), and assuming the 'femme' is the victim (Hassouneh & Glass, 2008, p. 322). Most importantly, research shows LGBTI people report unsupportive police responses more than the general public. Fifty-eight percent of respondents sought police assistance and felt supported in a Queensland study (Berman & Robinson, 2010), in contrast with 75% of the general public being satisfied with police (Australian Institute of Criminology [AIC], 2007). International research also suggests differential satisfaction with the police between LGBTI people and their heterosexual, cisgender counterparts (Dario et al., 2020; Gillespie, 2008; Miles-Johnson, 2015; Owen et al., 2017) which, in turn, might explain why, when victimised, LGBTI people are more likely to seek support from informal rather than formal networks such as the police (Kuehnle & Sullivan, 2003). These issues with reporting highlight the importance of exploring contextual factors, and the role of police liaison services in this landscape.

We have limited research specifically exploring the role of LGBTI police liaisons

Very little empirical research has examined LGBTI police liaison services in Australia, with available research being collected within broader studies on LGBTI victimisation (Berman & Robinson, 2010; Leonard et al., 2008). For example, Berman and Robinson (2010) conducted the largest ever study (n = 1094) of reporting homophobic and transphobic victimisation to police in Queensland. They found only 12% of the 53% victimised sought police assistance and of these only 4% sought support from LGBTI police liaison officers, with most noting the officers as supportive, although a few stated they felt unsupported. These low figures are remarkable considering 52% of respondents were aware of the availability of liaison officers. LGBTI communities expressed problems with LGBTI police liaison services, including high turnover, lack of availability of liaison officers, unrealistically large territories allocated to liaison officers, and lack of effective training, but interviews were not conducted with liaison officers to explore these concerns. This data is vital to ensure LGBTI victims are not 'receiving reduced support and a less valuable service' (Leonard et al., 2008, p. 42) than those seeking support from general police, and to increase the confidence of LGBTI people to report to police.

Methodology

This project sought to explore these concerns, aiming to provide detailed victim- and police-oriented analyses of the processes and practices of reporting LGBTI victimisation to police to address the gap between awareness and access of LGBTI police liaison programs. The project employed a mixed-methods approach to explore the localised, specific issues related to the context of LGBTI police liaison services. The methodology started with an online, structured questionnaire (marketed through a Facebook site and emails to LGBTI community organisations across all three states) targeting LGBTI people and invited them to complete an interview upon completing the questionnaire. When respondents had finished the questionnaire, they clicked a link directing them to a separate survey that recorded their contact details so these details were de-coupled from their questionnaire responses. The questionnaire data is not discussed in this paper so the focus of the methodological discussion below is the qualitative methodology.

In addition to interviewing LGBTI people, we also interviewed LGBTI police liaison officers. We approached these LGBTI police liaison officers through an email from the State Coordinators of LGBTI police liaison programs in each state. Semi-structured interviews with both key stakeholder groups were conducted in person or by phone by team members following a semi-structured interview schedule with a range of prompts, and audio-recorded interviews ranged from 30 to 60 minutes in duration. The project methodology underwent ethical review through the Queensland University of Technology, Griffith University, and the University of Sydney, and was administratively reviewed and approved by the research committees of police (Queensland Police Service, the New South Wales Police Force, and the Western Australian Police) and community organisations involved (ACON and Twenty10).

Forty-four ($n = 44$) LGBTI people expressed interest and were emailed by the research team. Ten ($n = 10$) LGBTI people from Queensland ($n = 7$) and New South Wales ($n = 3$) then replied to this email to arrange an interview. We had no expressions of interest to complete interviews with LGBTI people from Western Australia and none of the participants were aged 18 or under. Fifteen ($n = 15$) LGBTI police liaison officers expressed interest via email and interviews were conducted across Queensland ($n = 8$), New South Wales ($n = 5$), and Western Australia ($n = 2$).

All interviews were transcribed verbatim and the data were thematically coded using a three-step process. First, transcripts were uploaded into Leximancer text analysis software to generate key codes in the data. Second, these initial codes were used to structure the coding process using NVivo 10 qualitative data management program, with these codes constituting the core themes in the data. Third, the research team were divided in half into two smaller coding teams each comprised of two members, and one person from each of these teams conducted an initial thematic coding process with the data in NVivo. Each team had a separate NVivo database so we would not be influenced by how we each interpreted the data. When this process was complete, we moved onto member-checking each of the coded sets of data to support inter-coder reliability (Braun & Clarke, 2006; Vaismoradi, Jones, Turunen, & Snelgrove, 2016). We did not have a quantifiable process by which this was tested – we had an extended workshop where the two coding teams discussed their similarities and differences in their coding. Where our interpretations differed, we returned to the data to ensure that our interpretations aligned with the data set. From this point, we read and re-read the data to find sub-themes in the data set.

Key limitations informed the results of this study. First, the type of convenience sampling used limited the overall generalizability of the project. Although our preference would have been for a random sample, the mechanics of LGBTI people being a mostly unknown population in Australia meant that random sampling was not possible. Second, the sample sizes used in this project, and the responses we got from different participant pools were limited by the differences in the questions across jurisdictions. As different police organisations agreed to different types of questions, we were unable to conduct more thorough comparative analysis across the jurisdictions. Third, our sample was impacted by what the different jurisdictions did with their programs. For instance, as New South Wales Police focused on ensuring that every officer could support LGBTI people in their role, with all officers receiving some baseline training, we had insufficient numbers of people in that jurisdiction that had contacted liaison officers. In contrast, Queensland Police did not do this and we, therefore, had a lot of people that had contact with liaison officers in this jurisdiction. Finally, the uptake of the study in each state appeared to be influenced by whether or not we had someone on the ground in the state where the research was running. We had a significant response from New South Wales and Queensland, but very limited, if any, response to the survey and the interviews in Western Australia because we did not have a researcher on the ground in that jurisdiction to drive the project.

Results: the key themes emerging from the interviews

Interviews with key stakeholder groups confirmed what existing research had begun to elaborate: that LGBTI people do not have a lot of one to one contact with LGBTI police liaison officers (Berman & Robinson, 2010). All interviews with LGBTI liaison officers suggested that it was uncommon for LGBTI people to seek assistance from them directly. Officers noted how this happened 'not very often' (ML3NSW),[1] 'very rarely' (ML6QLD), 'once a year' (FL1QLD, ML1QLD), or up to 'half a dozen times a year' (FL2QLD, ML3QLD). It is unclear whether or not jurisdictions in Australia currently record statistics around the circumstances in which their LGBTI police liaison officers are deployed. Although the data demonstrated clearly that contact with LGBTI police liaison programs was minimal, data from the interviewees also demonstrated that multifarious, often conflicting issues created significant barriers that ultimately stopped LGBTI people from seeking support from LGBTI police liaison officers.

LGBTI police liaison officers are expected to be on the side of LGBTI people at all times

One of the greatest barriers noted by liaison officers was how 'when someone from the gay and lesbian community did utilise the service, they assumed you were always going to be on their side' (FL1NSW). Multiple examples of these types of situations were provided in interviews with these officers:

> Sometimes it's not about being gay, straight, bi, it's about you got the wrong idea or you're in the wrong or it's got nothing to do with your sexuality ... let's say a nightclub scene where someone is highly intoxicated has been thrown out of a night club or a licensed premises and they are trying to convince you ... that the only reason they have been kicked out is because they are gay ... when in fact it is because they are highly intoxicated, it has nothing to do with discrimination. (FL1NSW)

Another officer commented:

> One was a neighbourhood dispute from [SURBURB NAME REMOVED], some weird place that was way away. Basically, the officer there wasn't doing what he thought he should be doing but then you look at the occurrences there and there's like years' worth of false complaints between both neighbours and that sort of crap .... Basically, he wasn't happy with the response and he thought he'd ring me .... I've had friends that have had people saying, 'I want the LGBTI liaison officer' and I said, 'Well that's me.' 'Well you're not treating me the way you should ....' I'm like, 'You're still breaking the law ....' So it doesn't mean because I'm gay, you're then going to get off. (ML4QLD)

Liaison officers articulated an implicit expectation from LGBTI people that officers would necessarily support LGBTI people they were assisting, even when those people were breaching the law. This created considerable tensions between the desire to provide support to LGBTI people and the need to enforce the law: 'I've often said that I get more support from the police for being gay than I do from the community for being in the police' (ML2NSW). Interacting with a gay police liaison officer was assumed by members of the public to be their ticket out of doing something wrong. However, officers made it clear that this would not be the case. At other times, interviewees noted that it was not about doing something wrong that meant the LGBTI person could not be supported – it was rather about the lack of time these officers had to do their role: 'it's not because you are gay, it's because we are busy you know' (ML2QLD). Officers noted that members of the public often assumed that taking time to move through the processes of reporting a crime was discriminatory based on the amount of time it was taking.

Negative contemporary and historical police experiences stop LGBTI people going to liaisons

Negative past police experiences were a key concern influencing the willingness of LGBTI people to seek support from LGBTI police liaison officers. Importantly, past experiences included recent experiences they had and historical experiences they had heard about. Regardless of whether it was contemporary or historical, the interviewees made it abundantly apparent that negative interactions contributed to the development of negative perceptions of police, and subsequently less willingness to approach any police, including liaison officers. One interviewee noted that if they witnessed a New South Wales police officer 'being bashed, why, I would join in or hold the person's jacket so they don't get blood on themselves. I hate them' (GM3NSW).[2] Close to one-third of respondents in our study noted negative experiences including abuse, police misconduct, and discrimination. These experiences included assault and corruption (in two cases) and verbal abuse (in two cases), and some discussions about police officers not taking their reports seriously, or focusing issues that were not relevant to their report, which in one case included asking a victim of intimate partner violence about the purpose of sex toys rather than stopping the abuse they were experiencing (GM1QLD).

Not being taken seriously was a substantial issue for one participant subjected to years of sustained harassment from a neighbour. The interviewee stated police 'didn't believe me. They started with this position of doubt that this is harassment' (GM1NSW). The gay couple noted they were continually treated like they were over-reacting or told there was no evidence regarding the threats being made to them:

> I made a complaint about the way we were being treated, and the basis of my complaint was essentially that every time one of those events took place we went into a police station and the police wanted to regard it as a new event. I understand that this is what they are required to do. If our car had been spray-painted pink, which happened three to four times, the police would say that is just an instance of vandalism. And I would have to go through all the events over and over again to establish a history and explain to them why it wasn't just vandalism, why it was personally threatening, and why I did need their intervention. (GM1NSW)

There is no doubt that evidently negative experiences with police have heavily shaped how this person perceive police broadly, but importantly, they noted that the existence of the LGBTI police liaison program was unlikely to change how they viewed police regardless of the situation.

These ideas about police most certainly extended to historical mistrust of police. That is, historical negative experiences, regardless of whether they were personally experienced or heard about, meant that LGBTI people would not seek out support from liaison officers: 'Well, I think historical stuff is one. I don't think that applies to everyone, but historical interactions is one' (FL2QLD), with liaison officers noting that older LGBTI people still believe 'that we're all a bunch of assholes' (ML4QLD) and they therefore 'don't want to talk to coppers anyway' (ML3QLD):

> [A] lot of the issues that I was dealing with were older men and women who all had, if I can use the word, 'hang ups' from their treatment of police in the past or their perceptions of the police. Whereas it's not such an issue for younger people. (ML2QLD)

These attitudes were assumed to be widespread and evidenced by the critical response to police presence at Pride events or nightclub walkthroughs – LGBTI patrons assumed police were there to inflict violence in their safe spaces, rather than just to say hello (ML4QLD). Most importantly, if policing moments emerged that were reminiscent of historical violent policing practices with LGBTI people – such as the policing of Mardi Gras in 2013, where an officer violently arrested a gay male partygoer (see Rourke, 2013), relationships that police officers had forged with LGBTI people over many years were destroyed in an instant:

> I know a lot of police have been working for many, many years to try to break down all those bad images and build up trust ... that trust was, you know, taken away very quickly. And personally, like I said, I work very closely for years with the same type of people from different

> organisations, government and non-government councils and things like that and you go to meetings after that happened and they treat you differently all of a sudden and you think, "well you have known me for years." You know, so things like that are very hard. (FL2NSW)

Liaison officers interviewed made it abundantly clear that violent, discriminatory policing, reminiscent of (but perhaps not confined to) historical police-LGBTI interactions, still informs how LGBTI people think about and interact with police contemporaneously. Most importantly, these historical ideas would constitute a substantial barrier to service delivery with LGBTI police liaison programs because they continue to inform whether or not LGBTI people decide to seek support from liaison officers: if 'police still don't understand ... like transgender issues, why would I pick up the phone and have a conversation?' (ML3NSW).

LGBTI police liaison officers are perceived as no different from general police by LGBTI people

In this study, the very few LGBTI people that directly contacted LGBTI police liaison officers noted that interactions with these officers were not unlike dealing with general duties police officers. Some folks talked about how their experiences were not negative, but also 'not especially' (GM1NSW) positive because all officers were experienced as equally supportive. In other situations, interviewees recounted how unsatisfactory experiences emerged from interactions with LGBTI police liaison officers. In the example above where a gay couple were being subject to sustained harassment from a neighbour, the police handling of the process was immensely harmful. The couple 'would have to go through all the events over and over again ... [and] explain to them [police] why it wasn't just vandalism' (GM1NSW), and this process was repeated over and over again:

> [E]ven though I was going to the same station every time. And the disposition of the police is to not believe a victim when a victim says this is harassment and that goes for the GLLOS [Gay and Lesbian Liaison Officers] and every other police officer. That is where they let us down. (GM1NSW)

Although this process was repeated many times, the police still failed to believe he and his partner were being subject to sustained victimisation. What is even more disturbing is that this interviewee engaged in what he called 'filtering': where he and his partner went through an explicit decision-making process about what would be, and what would not be, reported to police, because they were concerned that reporting every incident of harassment to police would be a nuisance:

> I can't remember which point in that list of events, but at some point, we decided to report everything that happened. But even then, we filtered. So we can't report the mouth abuse at the shopping centre. You can't do that. He called me a poofter, well yes. And then you have to go into this long discussion of why it is offensive to be called a poofter. Yes, we did filter, and we said we don't want to be a nuisance. A piece of advice that I got from [NAME REMOVED] that was really interesting was, she said "I don't think you should go make a formal complaint because then you will just get everybody offside. You will enter a complaints process and everyone will be offside." (GM1NSW)

'Filtering' like this shows a clear disconnect between the priorities for the victim and the priorities for the police. There were many unreported incidents experienced by this gay couple because they did not want to be seen as a nuisance, and even those incidents reported were not understood by police as ongoing, sustained harassment and abuse, but rather as isolated incidents. This response certainly evidences well the importance of having all police trained to understand LGBTI issues and ensuring that police databases have the capacity to record narrative of ongoing harassment and abuse. Furthermore, it highlights the need to educate the public and police about the importance of reporting any incident of harassment to fully comprehend the ongoing nature of this form of abuse.

Two other interviewees noted similar views on liaison officers being no more helpful or supportive than general duties police officers, with one stating '[t]hey're just wallopers with a different name' (GM3NSW). Liaison officers were in fact characterised as worse than general police officers by one interviewee whose comments were informed by the experiences of one of their friends:

> I don't think it would make any difference. In fact, I've heard from this friend of mine that in fact they are worse. Those who are gay, treat gay people harder especially if they are closeted. It can be worse. If they are, it's like the reverse of them trying to show favouritism. Instead it can be worse. (GM2NSW)

While liaison officers did not have direct contact with this person, and the interviewee did not articulate how they came to think this way about liaison officers, he was not convinced that interacting with a police liaison officer would offer any more advantages than interacting with a general police officer, something that strongly suggests that all police officers require training about LGBTI issues.

Organisational structures and lack of police knowledge denied LGBTI people access to liaisons

Not being able to access a police liaison officer for advice was an ongoing issue noted by both LGBTI people and LGBTI police liaison officers: 'community people will come out and ask for a GLLO and a GLLO won't be on so they will walk out of the station' (ML2NSW). Information was provided by LGBTI police liaison officers about how police organisations were structured in ways that denied LGBTI people access to liaison officers. They noted how police rostering and shift systems meant LGBTI people could not access liaison officers due to 'being fobbed around' because 'accessibility is dismal' (FL1NSW). LGBTI people also talked about how their requests for access to police liaison officers had gone unactioned or were ignored by general police officers they were dealing with (GM3NSW, GM2NSW). Some participants raised the issue of how the programs lacked structure and formality in police organisations in ways that suggested they were of subsidiary importance because officers only trained as liaison officers on an 'as needed' basis. Officers suggested this would cause problems should a serious incident emerge involving a LGBTI person (ML5QLD).

There was significant frustration evidenced in the comments of LGBTI people that had unsuccessfully attempted to seek support from LGBTI police liaison officers. One lesbian female participant from Queensland recounted her experience of not being able to seek support with a liaison officer to report domestic violence: 'I did not get hold of a liaison officer, who I would be more comfortable talking to … I really wanted to be able to be dealing with the liaison officer, and they never returned my phone call' (LEF3QLD).

Interestingly, this participant later states that she questioned whether or not police reception had taken her seriously 'because I wasn't about to get thumped' (LE3QLD). Similar experiences were recounted by a gay male participant in New South Wales: 'there was very rarely one around, when I actually rang up and said can I speak to your GLLO they would say "she is not in today." ... I would leave a message to call me back and I wouldn't get much' (GM1NSW). The thoughts of liaison officers interviewed very much aligned with these sentiments:

> They ring back two days later and with our shifts particularly in the city they work two on, two off. So two 12-hour day shifts and then two 12-hour night shifts and then they go off for six. So if you are someone trying to contact a GLLO and they only have one at the command and you ring three times and each time I'm not there you might think that you're being fobbed (FL1NSW).

Ironically, some liaison officers interviewed even suggested that requesting a liaison officer thwarted good public service simply because the rostering and shift systems meant liaison officers were so difficult to access:

> "I would like to speak to a GLLO" and "Sorry they are not here." Now good customer service is, "Now can I help you." Now they have either left the station already, or if they get asked that next questions which they should, "Ah yes I want to report whatever, a domestic assault or whatever but I'm not comfortable talking to just anybody, can I see a GLLO?" "Oh now I understand," find out who it is, when they are on, find out if it is urgent. "Yes, it is urgent." "We don't have a GLLO on but there is senior detective out the back or there is a supervisor" ... we are here 24 hours a day we are dealing with stuff, everybody is trained to do things that's why sometimes the GLLO things can get in the way. (ML3NSW)

There is no doubt that further exploration is needed of how a service enhancement program, like LGBTI police liaison programs, are not actually enhancing service simply because of police rostering systems. All these examples evidence well the need to conduct further research on how police operational administration and management may be limiting the access that LGBTI people have to liaison officers, in addition to how these programs may be limiting the overall effectiveness of service provision.

Another issue raised was the lack of knowledge of general duties police officers about LGBTI police liaison programs, and how this lack of knowledge impacted on people being able to access these services. Ultimately, if officers did not have knowledge about these services, how were they going to know to refer LGBTI people on?

There were further examples where requests for liaison officers made by LGBTI people were expressly ignored by general duties police officers because they lacked knowledge of these programs, although this was an issue highlighted only by participants from New South Wales: 'There is no need for them at all because they don't seem to make a difference when you ask to see a GLLO they ignore you' (GM3NSW). Another commented,

> It is a load of PR. I don't know why the gay community actually needs specific LG liaison officers. When I was arrested for a so-called breach of an AVO against this drug dealer, I asked for a LG liaison officer [and] they ignored me (GM2NSW).

These issues were also highlighted by the liaison officers interviewed, with many noting how the lack of knowledge amongst general duties officers, about the programs and what services they offered, contributed to the overall invisibility of the LGBTI police liaison programs (Dwyer & Ball, 2020). Overall, they argued that if general police officers did not have knowledge of these programs, LGBTI people would not be provided with access to them when they needed this:

> It's not marketed, neither internally [n]or externally. I've had police say to me "Oh, I didn't even know liaison officers existed, what do you do?" I thought, "Well, not very much because no one calls us because no one knows about us!" (FL1QLD)

Another officer commented, 'I can pretty much guarantee that if I ring Police Link now and ask for a liaison officer, they wouldn't have a clue where to put me' (ML4QLD).

Both liaison officers and LGBTI people suggest that general duties police officers need to know and understand the services provided by LGBTI police liaison programs. If they lack this knowledge, this will sustain the ineffectiveness of the program, and this is a problem that requires amelioration by police organisations.

Only LGBTI-related issues should be reported to LGBTI police liaison officers

The degree to which LGBTI issues were linked to what was being reported had a significant influence on whether or not LGBTI people would seek support from LGBTI police liaison officers. Three interviewees, in Queensland and New South Wales, did not have past experiences with LGBTI police liaison officers precisely because they weighed up whether or not to seek support based on the relevance of the crime or issue to their sexuality (LE1QLD) and/or their gender identity (GQ1QLD). A key consideration in this process was whether LGBTI police liaison officers had the requisite understanding of the issues they needed support for:

> I think I would go there if I knew they existed, like I mean my cousin's transgender so she's, I would imagine if she had any problems or she got bashed up because of her life, I think she would definitely feel more comfortable going there, you know, especially when people knew her in high school as a guy, so like that's something more of a tense situation like that I think she would go, whereas I don't know depending on what happened why I would need to report something or go there (LE1QLD).

Another officer from Queensland added,

> I would have to know that they understood transgender and gender queer and let's say that I had been raped. I'd been vaginally raped; right now I don't think I would report that because I look like a dude. If I said that happened, there are a whole bunch of reasons I wouldn't report that. If that happened to me, but I looked like a dude but had both body parts I would worry they would continue to treat me a certain way and continue to use 'she' and see me as a woman. I would need to know that they understand transgender and that you can have X body parts but still be Y person and stuff like that (GQ1QLD).

A very careful, considered decision-making process is evidenced in these examples, with LGBTI people weighing up how much police liaison officers know (for instance, their knowledge of issues related to transgender experience), and therefore whether they are safe people to seek support from for their situation. These issues are also reflected in comments from LGBTI police liaison officers. Talking specifically about LGBTI people that attend a police station to report, male liaison 2 from Queensland contended that:

> It depends on the age of the person. The person I'm thinking of is in his 30s and he was quite shy ... going up to the front counter and stating domestic violence or assault. Or you have this young 20-year-old who didn't blink an eyelid, and he didn't care what they thought whether he was gay or whatever. Again, this is depending on your culture and where you're at. (ML2QLD)

These comments evidence the importance of all police, not just liaison officers, having some understanding of the issues impacting the lives of LGBTI people, and that we need to educate LGBTI people about this being incorporated into police training so they feel safe to seek support from, and report crime to, police.

Considering LGBTI people do not feel safe asking for assistance from liaison officers, we asked all interviewees about making sexuality and/or gender diversity a standard question to enhance police service, like the Indigenous standard question (Australian Institute of Health and Welfare (AIHW), 2010). Some stated this was undoubtedly important: 'Absolutely they should' (GM2QLD), but others suggested 'they should not be allowed,' then adding '[i]f it is relevant, yes, absolutely yes' (GM2NSW). Some participants suggested that their sexuality would be blatantly obvious to all police and there was therefore no need to ask: 'I don't care ... it's pretty obvious' (GM1NSW) and 'I wouldn't mind if they did because I am an openly gay person. But then I think, "why do people have to come out as gay?"' (GM2QLD). Overall, though, the responses from interviewees about this question were characterised by uncertainty – they vacillated between this being a useful and harmful strategy:

Respondent: It really depends on the context, and how it is relevant to what I was talking with the officer about.

Interviewer: So if there was a situation where you had been victimised and it was valid then, would you feel uncomfortable with an officer asking then?

Respondent: Depends on how they phrased it. If it was relevant, it was highly unlikely I would have offered the information. I'm perfectly capable of advocating for myself and giving the information by myself. (GQ1QLD)

Not all LGBTI interviewees were as comfortable as this interviewee about volunteering such information. It was no surprise, though, that agreement was much stronger about this concern when a discernible hate crime was involved:

> Absolutely they should. There should be, and I don't know because I've read reports about this, the need for this and I don't know if the police are currently keeping records on LGBT hate crimes but it needs to be recorded and it needs to be recorded how bad this problem is. This reminds me of another time where I was a victim down at Lismore, I had a Tropical Fruits stand and I was attacked quite badly and had to go to hospital for treatment and I asked for the police to attend and report it as – like the people were saying "you're a fucking poofter," to report it as a deliberate anti-gay attack .... It needs to be recorded, there needs to be stats to say that this community is being attacked. (GM2QLD)

Liaison officers also supported these ideas and argued that people would not report a crime that technically does not exist as a crime – such as hate crime – even if there are other things that the offenders might be charged with. Female liaison 1 in Western Australia (FL1WA) discussed an example of this situation: '[w]e had a guy that had the living bejesus beat out of him at a beat and he was with another guy and they [police organisation] still didn't see it as a homophobic hate crime.' If police had asked sensitive questions around sexuality and/or gender diversity in this instance, perhaps this might have had some chance of being recognised by police as a hate crime, and consequently this may encourage LGBTI people to report to police more often. Even though these questions have been previously raised in research (Dwyer, 2008), these issues are yet to be discussed due to the related ethical sensitivities.

Anonymity requests impact how much LGBTI police liaison officers can support LGBTI people

Anonymity was an issue identified by police liaison officers as shaping the decisions that LGBTI people make about reporting crimes to police. Views were clearly mixed about how often victims requested anonymity, but interviewees did recognise that anonymity was a factor influencing victim decisions to report or not. Participants stated that victims felt discomfort about providing personal details when discussing incidents with police as they are often simply requesting advice, and this limits the assistance that a liaison officer can provide (ML3QLD). Sometimes people requested anonymity in the first instance (ML4QLD), but in other situations, liaison officers suggested that it was more a situation where they 'don't push them' (ML3QLD). There was a key tension between not receiving much needed information, yet also gaining enough information to proceed with a report to assist the person. It was therefore a careful balancing act that liaison officers engaged in when interacting with LGBTI people. The degree of confidentiality was most often shaped by the type of situation being discussed:

> You know if you do know the identity of your victim it does take some coercion to turn their mind set around and make them to bat on so to speak, because if you push the barrel and you don't have a victim, you can't do anything about it. But if it is an incident where someone said on Oxford street between 10 [and] 2 in the morning there is a large group of men frequenting souped up cars and they come and give the guys a bad time as they are walking down the street to their cars, well sure that can be anonymous and you don't need to push it because some information is better than none. (FL1NSW)

While the type of situation shaped whether or not anonymity was possible for the officer above, other interviewees noted it was the trustworthiness of police with confidential information that was more likely to shape this. Even liaison officers argued that '[n]ot everybody is trustworthy in the police and what happens with the information' (ML1NSW). At other times, frustration was expressed by LGBTI people that did not want to share certain details, yet they simultaneously expected the liaison officers to do something: 'anonymous information, it is very hard. Someone comes into a police station and says, "I've been bashed up but I'm not going to tell you my name." That's not really going to work or go very far' (ML3NSW). Regardless of the situation, it is evident that anonymity creates significant tensions for both LGBTI people and liaison officers, with officers struggling to balance this concern with the need for information that enables the progression of a formal report.

Rules stop LGBTI police liaison officers from taking/investigating reports from LGBTI people and complicate supporting these people

A fundamental stipulation of liaison roles is that they are purely support roles, not investigative roles. At times, however, officers interviewed in this study noted they occasionally took reports depending on whether or not they had flexibility to do so from their supervisor: 'There's no reason why a manager can't be a little flexible' (FL1QLD). There were mixed feelings about doing this, though, with a range of factors related to policing work generally, and particularly policing LGBTI people, that informed these decisions. Some officers suggested the rules around this were restrictive and problematic, particularly in situations where they had built rapport and trust with a community member and they did not want to pass the situation on to another officer that may not follow up:

> You are just relying on other officers who you don't even know to continue doing the right thing with the investigation ... it just takes one officer to say the wrong thing or obviously not be interested or go through the motions and all that good work can be undone in a matter of seconds. (ML1QLD)

Others agreed with this, saying that once the initial complaint is made and identified as LGBTI-related, then 'I see benefit in forwarding the file to a LGBTI liaison officer for any follow-up and enforcement action of finalisation' (FL1QLD). Officers contended that police are now subject to so many accountability measures that '[i]t's not worth them losing their job or getting in trouble and [not] investigate it just because they might be homophobic or whatever ... [W]e're that accountable that they don't really have the choice to do a crap job' (ML4QLD). This, they argued, could restrict the effectiveness of the program.

Other officers thoughts departed from this as they noted that it was actually a practical consideration (ML4QLD) because there were times where 'someone else is more suited to investigate' (FL1NSW), in cases where it is 'a serious matter, so like a bodily harm or attempted murder' (ML3QLD), otherwise 'it'd be like me getting a motor mechanic to fix your refrigerator' (ML3QLD). At other times, it was as simple as liaison officers being 'snowed under' (ML4QLD) and lacking the time to address the situation. The issue can also be location-based where a liaison officer is not based in the location of the offence and ultimately liaison officers 'can't cut through the QPS police or constraints or procedures, just because someone is an LGBTI officer' (ML3QLD). Finally, some officers argued forcefully that moving into investigating a report profoundly shifted the dynamic of the liaison interaction, with the liaison role falling away: '[w]hen you do that, you lose that capacity to actually interact' (ML6QLD). This was an especial concern when a LGBTI person being supported was found to be at fault: 'those relationships that would have been established, have instantly been burned or getting burned because you no longer have that liaison capability' (ML6QLD). Not investigating any reports meant that a liaison could be firmly situated as being that person's advocate by making sure that proper processes are followed, and that issues are followed up and responded to appropriately (ML2QLD). The priority for this group, then, was definitely the type of policing job they were dealing with and who had the appropriate qualifications to do that policing work. A secondary consideration was whether or not the person was going to be better supported better by a liaison officer.

Lack of support from high-level police management for LGBTI Police liaison programs

One factor that dominated interviews with liaison officers in Queensland and Western Australia was 'the lack of support from the bosses' (ML5QLD). Officers were aware that high level management were not managing the program in effective ways and were '[v] ery pissed off' (FL1QLD), clearly noting that 'the frustration is with the organisation' (FL2QLD). Some officers admitted they were engaging in more tasks than they were paid for because they were doing the program coordinator role 'because no one else will do it and I don't want those relationships to slip away, basically' (ML4QLD). This had a range of flow-on effects that meant no funding or resources, and no time (ML4QLD; ML5QLD; FL1QLD; FL2QLD), all factors that prevented enthusiastic liaison officers from realising new program ideas (FL1NSW; ML3QLD; FL1QLD). Frustration was particularly directed at senior police management when permission for liaison officers to march in the Mardi Gras was not forthcoming, and how this subsequently demonstrated a message of non-support that made their job difficult (ML5QLD). Others made it clear they needed additional training to ensure their effectiveness as a liaison (ML4NSW; ML5QLD), and they needed additional time to maintain their LGBTI community networks (ML4NSW), with some officers doing this work in their own time (ML4QLD; ML5QLD). All these issues were identified as needing improvement to ensure the overall effectiveness of liaison programs.

Discussion

A number of key issues have emerged from our study that provide important indications of how police organisations might move forward with LGBTI police liaison programs. First, it is clear that LGBTI people had an awareness of these liaison services, even if this awareness included misunderstanding about their role. Despite having this awareness, though, LGBTI people were not using these services to report and seek support as other research has found (Berman & Robinson, 2010). Importantly, this does not mean liaison services have no value – liaison officers interviewed argued strongly that simply having these services exist is as important as having them used. These services signal to LGBTI communities that police organisations recognise the queer diversity of communities and police (Colvin, 2012b). They provide meaningful demonstrations of policing as they align with procedural justice and police legitimacy (Dario et al., 2020; Mazerolle, Bennett, Davis, Sargeant, & Manning, 2013), where respectful, thoughtful policing, regardless of the outcome for the person involved, can be exemplified both externally and internally with police organisations. Most importantly, liaison services are yet to be full realised because investment by police organisations in these programs differs so widely, as other research has found (Tobler, 2006), and lack of visibility impacts who knows about them (Dwyer & Ball, 2020). With full support and solid investment, the programs could potentially be much more effective, and only then will be able to measure effectiveness of more siloed police service enhancement programs set up to support vulnerable people (Asquith & Bartkowiak-Theron, 2014).

Second, barriers like not feeling issues are important enough, and not feeling comfortable to report because of lack of anonymity, are not new – they inform policing across all communities. However, in the LGBTI liaison role, these issues are exacerbated and complicated by existing attitudes about LGBTI folks both within and outside of police (Miles-Johnson, 2013b; Myers, Forest, & Miller, 2004), and how LGBTI folks think about the seriousness of their issue (i.e. verbal abuse not being reported because they might be interpreted as a nuisance by police when it happened and was reported so often). Our data suggests that police reporting systems need change to recognise that multiple and ongoing incidents can exemplify a sustained pattern of abusive behaviour. This might lessen the vicarious trauma reported by our participants that came from retelling histories of abuse to each new police officer. They might also feel better supported simply because all incidents were considered important enough to be recorded in police records. This also points to the potential utility of establishing third-party reporting mechanisms so that people can anonymously report what might be patterned abusive behaviours for analysis by police.

Third, LGBTI police liaison roles clearly serve a role in breaking down homophobia and transphobia in policing organisations. Liaison officers noted one of the most important roles involved educating other officers about these issues, a form of 'training' which is perhaps yet to be articulated in existing research focused on the effectiveness of targeted sensitivity training (Israel, Harkness, Delucio, Ledbetter, & Avellar, 2014). This did not extend to overall internal communication (and managerial support) related to these programs with police organisations – it is abundantly evident that further communication work is needed to showcase the availability and value of liaison officers. External impacts of the role are also less clear and our research indicates the need for clearer communication with LGBTI people about what liaison officers can and cannot do.

Finally, precariousness certainly influences LGBTI police liaison programs and this is experienced by officers and LGBTI people. Relationships between police and LGBTI communities are heavily shaped by their contact with general duties officers – they are the officers that LGBTI people most commonly deal, something which indicates that all police officers ought to have specialist knowledge about LGBTI issues. Further, it highlights how siloed specialised liaison programs can mean problematic policing experiences with limited impact, but these programs need more time and investment before we can confidently make this claim. Liaison officers and LGBTI people in our study agreed that these programs were vital for supporting LGBTI victims, offenders, or witnesses. Our study shows that, until LGBTI police liaison programs are provided with sustained and sufficient investment and support by police organisations, we will not truly comprehend the relationship-building work they do with LGBTI people and how they support them to report to police.

Conclusion

The climate in which LGBTI police liaison programs exist and function is complicated and challenging. Significant barriers exist which are keenly felt by both LGBTI people and LGBTI police liaison officers. Even so, these programs represent important positive symbols of LGBTI-police relationship building and indicate support for LGBTI people in many ways. Measuring the very complex full impact of these service enhancement programs, however, cannot be actioned at this point when these programs clearly need more time to establish themselves to ensure we can capture a clear sense of how they best support LGBTI people in their relationships with police. We can only speculate about whether the critical influence of liaison programs is the internal process officers engage with in promoting more appropriate and sensitive policing to vulnerable communities, and broadly educating these officers in new directions. Alternatively, we are yet to understand comprehensively whether their role is instead one of making police organisations more approachable, and therefore more supportive, for LGBTI people, regardless of their status as victim or offender. What is abundantly clear at this point is how police organisations need to consistently invest in and support their LGBTI police liaison programs if they are to be effective in any way at all, and that this high-level support and investment happens within a culture where efforts are being made to eradicate suspicion, mistrust, and problematic attitudes between LGBTI people and police.

Notes

1. The letters and numbers following quotes from liaison officers indicate the sex of the participant, the fact that they are a liaison officer, the number of the participant, and the state in which they work. Thus, ML3NSW is the third male liaison officer from New South Wales interviewed. FL1QLD is the first female liaison officer from Queensland interviewed, and so on.
2. The quotes from LGBTI people interviewed are referenced in a similar way to those from liaison officers above; the first letters refer to the participants' sexuality and/or gender identification, the numbers to the number of the interview, and the final letters to the state of the participant. However, to distinguish between liaison and lesbian, the letters 'LE' are used to identify lesbian women.

Disclosure statement

No potential conflict of interest was reported by the authors.

ORCID

Angela Dwyer http://orcid.org/0000-0001-5152-7222
Matthew Ball http://orcid.org/0000-0002-2326-5752
Murray Lee http://orcid.org/0000-0003-2220-0313
Christine Bond http://orcid.org/0000-0003-0429-5208

References

American Civil Liberties Union. (2017). Why *sodomy laws matter*. Retrieved from https://www.aclu.org/other/why-sodomy-laws-matter

Amnesty International. 2005. *Stonewalled: Police abuse and misconduct against LGBT people in the United States*. Washington, DC: Author. Retrieved from https://www.amnesty.org/download/Documents/84000/amr511222005en.pdf

Asquith, N., & Bartkowiak-Theron, I. (2014). Policing diversity and vulnerability in the post-Macpherson era: Unintended consequences and missed opportunities. *Policing*, *9*(1), 89–100.

Attorney General's Department of New South Wales. (2003). *You shouldn't have to hide to be safe: A report on homophobic hostilities and violence against gay men and lesbians in New South Wales*. Sydney: Attorney General's Department of NSW.

Australian Institute of Criminology (AIC). (2007). *Community satisfaction with police*. Crime Facts Info No. 161. Canberra: Australian Institute of Criminology.

Australian Institute of Health and Welfare (AIHW). (2010). *National best practice guidelines for collecting indigenous status in health data sets*. Canberra: Australian Government.

Bartkowiak-Theron, I., & Asquith, N. (2012). The extraordinary intricacies of policing vulnerability. *Australasian Policing: A Journal of Professional Practice and Research*, *4*(2), 43–49.

Berman, A., & Robinson, S. (2010). *Speaking out: Stopping homophobic and transphobic abuse in Queensland*. Brisbane: Australian Academic Press.

Berrill, K.T. (1992). Anti-gay violence and victimization in the United States: An overview. In G. M. Herek & K.T. Berrill (Eds.), *Hate crimes: Confronting violence against lesbians and gay men* (pp. 19–45). Newbury Park: Sage.

Braun, V., & Clarke, V. (2006). Using thematic analysis in psychology. *Qualitative Research in Psychology*, *3*(2), 77–101.

Briones-Robinson, R., Powers, R.A., & Socia, K.M. (2016). Sexual orientation bias crime: Examination of reporting, perception of police bias, and differential police response. *Criminal Justice and Behavior*, *43*(12), 1688–1709.

Colvin, R.A. (2012a). *Gay and lesbian cops: Diversity and effective policing*. Colorado: Lynne Rienner Publishers.

Colvin, R.A. (2012b). Improved policing in an invisible community: A case study of the gay and lesbian liaison unit of Washington DC. In R. Schwester (Ed.), *Handbook of critical incident analysis* (pp. 303–315). New York, NY: ME Sharpe/Taylor & Francis.

Copple, J.E., & Dunn, P.M. (2017). *Gender, sexuality, and 21st century policing: Protecting the rights of the LGBTQ+ community*. Washington, DC: Office of Community Oriented Policing Services.

Couch, M., Pitts, M., Mulcare, H., Croy, S., Mitchell, A., & Patel, S. (2007). *Tranznation: A report on the health and wellbeing of transgendered people in Australia and New Zealand*. Melbourne: Gay and Lesbian Health Victoria and The Australian Research Centre in Sex, Health and Society. Retrieved from http://www.glhv.org.au/files/Tranznation_Report.pdf

Dario, L., Fradella, H.F., Verhagen, M., & Parry, M.M. (2020). Assessing LGBT people's perceptions of police legitimacy. *Journal of Homosexuality, 67*(7), 885–915.

Dwyer, A. (2008). Policing queer bodies: focusing on queer embodiment in policing research as an ethical question. *QUT Law Review, 8*(2), 414–428.

Dwyer, A. (2014). Pleasures, perversities, and partnerships: The historical emergence of LGBT-police relationships. In D. Peterson & V.R. Panfil (Eds.), *The handbook of LGBT communities, crime, and justice* (pp. 149–164). New York, NY: Springer.

Dwyer, A., & Ball, M. (2013, July). GLBTI police liaison services: A critical analysis of existing literature. *Proceedings of The Australian and New Zealand Critical Criminology Conference 2012* (pp. 11–18), Hobart. Retrieved from http://www.utas.edu.au/tiles/publications_and_reports/conference_proceedings/The%206th%20Annual%20Australian%20and%20New%20Zealand%20Critical%20Criminology%20Conference%20Proceedings%202012.pdf

Dwyer, A., & Ball, M.J. (2020). "You'd just cop flak from every other dickhead under the sun": Navigating the tensions of (in)visibility and hypervisibility in LGBTI police liaison programs in three Australian states. *Journal of Contemporary Criminal Justice, 36*(2), 274–292.

Fradella, H.F., & Grundy, K. (2016). The criminal regulation of sex: The limits of morality and consent. In H.F. Fradella & J. Sumner (Eds.), *Sex, law, and (in)justice* (pp. 183–215). New York, NY: Routledge.

Gillespie, W. (2008). Thirty-five years after Stonewall: An exploratory study of satisfaction with police among gay, lesbian, and bisexual persons at the 34th annual Atlanta pride festival. *Journal of Homosexuality, 55*(4), 619–647.

Groombridge, N. (1999). Perverse criminologies: The closet of Doctor Lombroso. *Social & Legal Studies, 8*(4), 531–548.

Harry, J. (1990). Conceptualizing anti-gay violence. *Journal of Interpersonal Violence, 5*(3), 350–358.

Hassouneh, D., & Glass, N. (2008). The influence of gender role stereotyping on women's experiences of female same-sex intimate partner violence. *Violence against Women, 14*(3), 310–325.

Herek, G.M., Cogan, J.C., & Gillis, J.R. (2002). Victim experiences in hate crimes based on sexual orientation. *Journal of Social Issues, 58*(2), 319–339.

Hillier, L., Jones, T., Monagle, M., Overton, N., Gahan, L., Blackman, J., & Mitchell, A. (2010). *Writing themselves in 3: The third national study on the sexual health and wellbeing of same sex attracted and gender questioning young people.* Melbourne: La Trobe University, Australian Research Centre in Sex, Health and Society.

Hunter, J. (1990). Violence against lesbian and gay male youths. *Journal of Interpersonal Violence, 5* (3), 295–300.

Israel, T., Harkness, A., Delucio, K., Ledbetter, J.N., & Avellar, T.R. (2014). Evaluation of police training on LGBTQ issues: Knowledge, interpersonal apprehension, and self-efficacy. *Journal of Police and Criminal Psychology, 29*(2), 57–67.

Kuehnle, K., & Sullivan, A. (2003). Gay and lesbian victimisation: Reporting factors in domestic violence and bias Incidents. *Criminal Justice and Behaviour, 30*(1), 85–96.

Lambda Legal. (2015). *Protected and served? Survey of LGBT/HIV contact with police, courts, prisons, and security.* Retrieved from https://www.lambdalegal.org/protected-and-served

Leonard, W., Mitchell, A., Patel, S., & Fox, C. (2008). *Coming forward: The underreporting of heterosexist violence and same sex partner abuse in Victoria.* Melbourne: Australian Centre for Sex, Health and Society. Retrieved from http://www.latrobe.edu.au/arcshs/assets/downloads/reports/ComingForwardReport.pdf

Mallory, C., Hasenbush, A., & Sears, B. (2015). *Discrimination and harassment by law enforcement officers in the LGBT community.* https://williamsinstitute.law.ucla.edu/wp-content/uploads/LGBT-Discrimination-and-Harassment-in-Law-Enforcement-March-2015.pdf

Mason, G. (1993). Violence against lesbians and gay men. *Violence Prevention Today* No. 2. Canberra: Australia Institute of Criminology. Retrieved from https://pdfs.semanticscholar.org/6822/e8eac99a7d17843ab62e2a348acb19767acc.pdf

Mazerolle, L., Bennett, S., Davis, J., Sargeant, E., & Manning, M. (2013). Legitimacy in policing: A systematic review. *Campbell Systematic Reviews, 2013*(1), 1–147.

Miles-Johnson, T. (2013a). LGBTI variations in crime reporting: How sexual identity influences decisions to call the cops. *Sage Open, 2013*(2), 1–15.

Miles-Johnson, T. (2013b). Confidence and trust in police: How sexual identity difference shapes perceptions of police. *Current Issues in Criminal Justice*, *25*(2), 685–702.

Miles-Johnson, T. (2015). "They don't identify with us": Perceptions of police by Australian transgender people. *International Journal of Transgenderism*, *16*(3), 169–189.

Myers, K., Forest, K., & Miller, S. (2004). Officer Friendly and the tough cop: Gays and lesbians navigate homophobia and policing. *Journal of Homosexuality*, *47*(1), 17–37.

Out to Protect. (2016). *Every agency needs an LGBT liaison*. Retrieved from https://www.comingoutfrombehindthebadge.com/commentary/agency-lgbt-liaison/

Owen, S.S., Burke, T.W., Few-Demo, A.L., & Natwick, J. (2017). Perceptions of the police by LGBT communities. *American Journal of Criminal Justice*. Advance online publication. doi:10.1007/s12103-017-9420-8

Pattavina, A., Hirschel, D., Buzawa, E., Faggiani, D., & Bentley, H. (2007). A comparison of the police response to heterosexual versus same-sex intimate partner violence. *Violence against Women*, *13*(4), 374–394.

Peel, E. (1999). Violence against lesbians and gay men: Decision-making in reporting and not reporting crime. *Feminism & Psychology*, *9*(2), 161–167.

Rourke, A. (2013, March 5). Police brutality alleged at Sydney Gay Mardi Gras. *The Guardian*. Retrieved from https://www.theguardian.com/world/2013/mar/06/police-brutality-gay-mardi-gras1

Russell, E.K. (2020). *Queer histories and the politics of policing*. London: Routledge.

Seabrook, M. (1992). Homosexuality and the police. *New Law Journal*, *4*(2), 325–326.

Skilling, L. (2016). Community policing in Kenya: The application of democratic policing principles. *The Police Journal: Theory, Practice and Principles*, *89*(1), 3–17.

Tobler, A. (2006). "We do general policing": Sexuality in the Gay and Lesbian Liaison Unit of the Metropolitan Police Department, Washington, DC. *Graduate Journal of Social Science*, *3*(2), 1–92.

Tomsen, S. (2009). *Violence, prejudice and sexuality*. New York: Routledge.

Vaismoradi, M., Jones, J., Turunen, H., & Snelgrove, S. (2016). Theme development in qualitative content analysis and thematic analysis. *Journal of Nursing Education and Practice*, *6*(5), 100–110.

Williams, M.L., & Robinson, A.L. (2004). Problems and prospects with policing the lesbian, gay, and bisexual community in Wales. *Policing & Society*, *14*(3), 213–232.

Wolff, K., & Cokely, C. (2007). "To protect and to serve?": An exploration of police conduct in relation to the gay, lesbian, bisexual, and transgender community. *Sexuality & Culture*, *11*(2), 1–23.

An act of terror and an act of hate: national elite and populace newspaper framing of pulse nightclub shooting

Jace L. Valcore and Kevin Buckler

ABSTRACT

The Pulse nightclub mass shooting is a defining event for the LGBTQ and Latinx communities. It signified that much remains to be done to achieve true equality and equitable treatment over and above the symbolic mentions of it in law and public policy. The news media is an important mechanism for communication of meaning following tragic and painful events such as the Pulse shooting. This study examined how the Pulse nightclub shooting that occurred on 12 June 2016, was covered by influential national newspapers in the United States, *The New York Times, The Washington Post*, and *USA Today*, to determine how the event was framed, what types of sources were relied upon, and what types of social and legal solutions were emphasized. The unit of analysis was direct and indirect quotes in each news article. Content analysis revealed that the dominant framing of the attack was that of a terrorist act committed by a pathological, ideologically motivated offender. The most common control mechanism discussed were soft measures, particularly gun control. Little attention was given to the victims or the anti-LGBTQ nature of the shooting.

In the middle of Pride month, on 12 June 2016, a 29-year-old Afghani-American man shot 102 patrons of a popular LGBTQ nightclub, Pulse, in Orlando, Florida with a legally purchased semi-automatic rifle and handgun. Forty-nine victims died in the attack; 22 were Puerto Rican, and nearly all were Latinx and LGBTQ (lesbian, gay, bisexual, transgender, queer). Police shot and killed the offender, Omar Mateen, following a three-hour standoff. During the attack, Mateen placed three calls to 911 in which he expressed anger directed at the United States for military bombings and interference in the Middle East, and he claimed allegiance to the Islamic State of Iraq and Syria (ISIS), a jihadist militant group also known as the Islamic State of Iraq and the Levant (ISIL) (see Mabon & Royle, 2016). At the time of the attack it was the deadliest mass shooting in United States history, but was surpassed one year later by a more lethal mass shooting that occurred at a concert in Las Vegas (Montero, 2019). The Pulse shooting in Orlando remains as the deadliest incident of violence against LGBTQ and Latinx people in United States history (Dastiger, 2017).

It appeared to many observers that news coverage of the Pulse shooting was focused primarily on the offender and his extremist, Islamist motivations, and gave considerably less attention to the victims and to perceptions of the attack as one of homophobic aggression that extended beyond religious or nationalistic ideology (see Ferguson, 2018). There was considerable discussion and debate about how to define the incident and the offender, and how policy makers should respond, but little focus on the consequences of the shooting for the victims and their communities. The significance of the attack for LGBTQ people around the world, the Puerto Rican community, and the wider Latinx community, was overshadowed by the offender's self-professed Muslim background and allegiance to the Islamic State (La Fountain-Stokes, 2018). While there has been narrative, there has been little empirical research exploring or analyzing news coverage of the Pulse shooting.

Terror, hate, or both: why it matters

Mass shootings, acts of terrorism, and hate crime incidents have all increased in frequency and severity in the United States over the past few years. Reported hate crimes, as tallied in the FBI's Uniform Crime Report (2018), have steadily increased each year since 2015; including a 17% increase from 2016 to 2017. Mass shootings, defined as incidents in which four or more people are shot at a single time and space, have also steadily increased each decade since the 1970s (Krouse & Richardson, 2015). Similarly, incidents of domestic terrorism, particularly far-right extremist violence, have been on the rise. The number of far-right terrorist attacks in the United States more than quadrupled from 2016 to 2017 (Jones, 2018). These reports and statistics are complicated, though, by the fact and/or perception that many incidents of mass shooting, domestic terrorism, or hate crime, may be one and the same, but distinctions made by the media and the legal system have important ramifications.

Defining terrorism and hate crime

The Federal Bureau of Investigation (FBI) defines domestic terrorism as 'acts of violence that [violate] the criminal laws of the United States or any state, committed by individuals or groups without any foreign direction, and appear to be intended to intimidate or coerce a civilian population, or influence the policy of a government by intimidation or coercion, and occur primarily within the territorial jurisdiction of the United States' (Bjelopera, 2016, para.1). A domestic terrorist is motivated by a U.S. based political or religious ideology, such as anti-abortion extremism or white supremacy (Bjelopera, 2016; FBI, 2019), and is typically a minority-group member targeting the majority or dominant group in an 'upward crime' (Black, 2004). Recently, federal agencies have focused on the 'lone wolf' terrorist, or 'homegrown violent extremist.' According to the Department of Homeland Security and the FBI, a homegrown violent extremist (HVE) is a person who lives or operates primarily in the United States, but is motivated by ideologies and objectives of foreign terrorist organizations (Bjelopera, 2016). The distinction is simply that a homegrown extremist is influenced in some manner by a foreign terrorist ideology rather than a domestic ideology.

Hate crimes and domestic terrorism both fall under the purview of the Federal Bureau of Investigation, though most hate crime prosecutions are initiated at the state level. The Hate Crime Statistics Act[1] defines hate crimes as 'crimes that manifest evidence of prejudice based on race, gender and gender identity, religion, disability, sexual orientation, or ethnicity, including where appropriate the crimes of murder, non-negligent manslaughter; forcible rape; aggravated assault; simple assault; intimidation; arson; and destruction, damage or vandalism of property.' Hate crime is a social construct, which lends itself to imprecise definitions. Two key components of hate crime that have broad consensus include the bias or prejudice of the offender and the social identity of the victim (Jacobs & Potter, 1998).

The prevailing assumption is that hate crime offenders are motivated by personal malice and prejudice. The offenses, described as 'downward crimes,' are frequently committed by majority group members against minority group members as a way of asserting social control and dominance (Deloughery, King, & Asal, 2012). According to extant research and statistics, a 'typical' hate crime involves an unplanned assault upon a racial, religious, or sexual/gender minority by a group of young, white, males without connections to an organized hate group or specific ideological motivation (Deloughery et al., 2012; McDevitt, Levin, & Bennett, 2002); they are often first time offenders, and there is often alcohol involved (Gerstenfeld, 2018).

Hate crimes and the LGBTQ community

Members of the LGBTQ community are disproportionately targeted for violence, harassment, and discrimination based upon their real or perceived gender and sexual minority status, as well as intersecting racial and economic statuses (Buist & Lenning, 2016; Meyer, 2015). Gay males and transgender women of color, in particular, face consistently high rates of violent hate crime victimization, including homicide and police abuse (Meyer, 2015; Mogul, Ritchie, & Whitlock, 2011; Tillery, Ray, Cruz, & Waters, 2018). While most hate crimes are violent and tend to be more violent than non-hate motivated assaults, anti-LGBTQ hate crimes are the most severe, even when committed by a single offender rather than a group, which is more common for hate crimes and increases the level of physical injury to victims (Lantz & Kim, 2019).

Hate crime laws were originally a bipartisan policy issue that allowed for both 'tough on crime' politicians and those concerned with the civil rights of minority groups to feel that they were addressing the social problem of bias and prejudice-motivated violence (Jacobs & Potter, 1998). But, they have been criticized as a form of identity politics that inflames inter-group conflict (Jacobs & Potter, 1998), and critiqued for failing to address or solve the root causes of hate crime (Gerstenfeld, 2018; Valcore & Dodge, 2019). Scholars have also specifically argued that hate crime laws may actually be harmful to the LGBTQ community because they only serve to strengthen a punitive criminal legal system that historically and continually mistreats and abuses minorities, particularly those with intersecting racial/ethnic and LGBTQ identities (Mogul, Ritchie & Whitlock, 2011; Meyer, 2014). Meyer (2015) further noted that the typical conception of an anti-LGBTQ hate crime is one in which a privileged, white, gay, male is randomly attacked simply because of his sexuality (i.e. Matthew Shepard) and that this 'stranger danger' stereotype fails to consider that victims and offenders of hate crime cross multiple lines of group identity, including class, race, and gender. It is extremely difficult for a Hispanic gay man or a black transgender woman to clearly define a violent attack against them as one based solely upon race, or sexuality, or gender, which prevents recognition and support from the criminal justice system.

Distinguishing between domestic terrorism and hate crime

While the typical hate crime is opportunistic and lacks connection to a hate group or specific ideology (Deloughery et al., 2012; McDevitt et al., 2002), it is notable that hate crime and domestic terror have commonalities. Both are intended to intimidate and wreak terror on an entire group, and both include targets selected because of their identity. A research brief from The National Consortium for the Study of Terrorism and Responses to Terrorism concluded 'that hate crime and terrorism are more alike than different,' and that increases in one often results in increases in the other, particularly when far-right extremism is the cause (2016, p. 2). Gerstenfeld (2018) similarly noted that hate crime offenders and domestic terrorists share demographic and social characteristics in that they are almost all young men with access to guns who have been socially isolated and influenced by extremist ideology. For investigators, distinguishing between personal malice and ideologically motivated actions may be difficult, because they must rely on what can be proven in court (i.e. the suspect's expressed motivation): did the suspect articulate a foreign ideology, use racist slurs, belong to a hate group, or express extremist ideology on social media?

To further illustrate, consider that the majority of mass public shooters in the United States are white, male, American citizens (Duwe, 2007), yet there has been inconsistent and politicized use of the term 'terrorism.' The 'terrorist' label is one that appears to be reserved for non-white offenders (Beydoun, 2018; Norris, 2017). Dylann Roof, a young white supremacist, motivated by a desire to provoke a 'race war', killed 9 Black/African American people who were attending a church bible study (qtd. in Norris, 2017, p. 503). Legal analysis by Norris (2017) indicates that the crime was clearly domestic terrorism under federal law. Roof was motivated by a U.S. based, racist ideology (FBI, 2019). Yet, he was tried and convicted on federal hate crime charges (possibly because domestic terrorism is a category and not a prosecutable offense). The FBI investigated Mateen, however, as a 'homegrown violent extremist' who committed an act of terrorism (Hauslohner, Achenbach, & Nakashima, 2016).

The grey area between domestic terrorism and hate crime allows for suspects with links to domestic terrorist ideologies to be charged with hate crimes. It is unclear to what extent this influences how the government understands the threat posed by domestic extremism, but recent reports indicate that the Trump administration is failing to seriously address it (Clark, 2019). Forty-two law enforcement officers have been murdered by domestic extremists since 2005 (Hodges & Sommerstein, 2018) and the majority of current FBI domestic terrorism investigations involve white supremacist motivations. Following the federal arrest of 57 members of a white supremacist group in April 2018, Attorney General Jeff Sessions stated that 'Not only do white supremacist gangs subscribe to a repugnant, hateful ideology, they also engage in significant, organized and violent criminal activity' (qtd, in Jones, 2018, p. 6). And yet, news media spend considerably more time covering foreign terrorist groups, fueling Islamophobia and xenophobia. Kearns, Betus, and Lemieux (2019) found that terrorist attacks with Muslim perpetrators received, on average, 357% more news coverage than attacks with non-Muslim offenders. Like 9/11, the Pulse shooting was followed by attacks on mosques and an increase in harassment and violence against people across the country who were or were perceived to be Muslim (Hauser & Blinder, 2016; St. George, 2016), but news reports indicated that heightened security concerns following the attack were centered on gay bars and Pride parades, not on mosques or the Muslim community (e.g. Halzak, Hui, O'Connell, 2016).

A significant distinction between an event labeled a hate crime and one perceived to be an act of terrorism is the resulting recognition of the victims (or lack thereof) and the response from community members, officials, and elected representatives. Hate crimes are committed against a specifically identifiable social group, such as the LGBTQ community, while acts of terrorism are committed against 'all of us.' LGBTQ victims of violence are frequently blamed and shamed for their victimization, and are frequently mistreated by police and other authorities (Buist & Lenning, 2016; Meyer, 2015). Many politicians and commentators tried to claim that the Pulse attack was an attack on America, on all its citizens, effectively ignoring the obvious fact that the target was a gay nightclub, not a generic public space, and that the victims were Latinx and LGBTQ, not privileged majority group members. A society's failure to properly recognize the harm done to the members of an oppressed community by failing to accurately label a crime against them prevents legal recognition, negates their experience, and reinforces the offender's message that they should be erased (Lawrence, 2016).

Framing terror and hate: the role of the news media

Scholars have long studied and oft lamented the influence of the news media upon individual and societal perceptions of crime and social deviance as well as the justice system that responds to it (Potter & Kappeler, 2006). News media give disproportionate attention to crime and violence. While terrorism is responsible for less than 0.01% of deaths in the United States, it constituted 35.6% of *The New York Times*' coverage (based on article mentions) in 2016 (Ritchie, 2019). Similarly, homicide is the cause of less than 1% of deaths in the United States, but received nearly 23% of the coverage in the *Times* (Ritchie, 2019). Previous studies have determined that news media rely heavily on official sources of information on crime, such as law enforcement, rather than academics or expert scholars (Buckler, Griffin, & Travis, 2008). Furthermore, those official sources emphasize individual pathology as the cause of crime, rather than examining social factors, and point to hard control measures, such as retribution and deterrence, rather than soft control measures like rehabilitation or treatment (Welch, Fenwick, & Roberts, 1998).

The news media often frame crime, social deviance, and terrorism stories through political and ideological lenses that emphasize the views of political leaders, blame individuals, scapegoat minorities, and fail to acknowledge systemic issues or social influences on criminal behavior (Brinson, & Stohl, 2009; Chagnon, 2015). Brinson and Stohl's (2009) study of how terrorism is presented in the press of the United States and the United Kingdom showed that the differential direction of the coverage corresponded to how political leaders discussed terrorism. Notably, Powell's (2011) analysis found that since 9/11, United States media have framed international terrorists as members of Muslim/Arab/Islam organized terror cells working against 'Christian America,' while domestic terrorists are portrayed as a minor threat and as 'troubled individuals' (p. 91).

Exceptionally violent hate crimes tend to gain substantial media and political attention, such as the brutal murders of Matthew Shepard and James Byrd, Jr. in 1998. Ott and Aoki (2002) analyzed coverage of the Shepard murder in Wyoming in three nationally influential newspapers (*New York Times, Los Angeles Times, Washington Post*), *Time* magazine, and *The*

Advocate. They identified four distinct themes: naming the event, making the event a political symbol, expunging the evil within, and restoring the social order. Generally, the media first attempted to define and label the event, used the victim's status to fuel emotion and gain attention, identified and named an individual culprit, and finally, suggested a path to restore peace and order to the affected communities. Husselbee and Elliott (2002) conducted a more expansive analysis of both national and regional news media framing of hate crime, including both Shepard and the James Byrd, Jr. homicide that occurred in Jasper, Texas. News media coverage of both homicides centered on the community in which it occurred and its citizens, the image and the attention that the town received due to the murder, as well as community attitudes about race or sexuality.

The dominant framing of these two crimes was that they were anomalies committed by lone offenders temporarily disrupting the social order in otherwise peaceful and tolerant communities (Husselbee & Elliott, 2002). As noted by Lewis (2014), this emphasis on extreme crimes obscures the more ordinary hate crimes and instances of discrimination which occur daily. Lewis (2014) also observed that press coverage in the 21st century has moved from reporting on hate crimes to offering commentary and debating whether or not certain crimes warrant the hate crime label. Even the excessively violent murders of transgender women of color which occur with alarming frequency receive little national media attention today, and newspaper coverage frequently misgenders and misrepresents the victims (Waters, Jindasurat, & Wolfe, 2016).

Public discourse and media coverage of hate crimes, like that concerning mass shooters and domestic terrorists, frequently blames the hatred and prejudice of the individual offender, effectively absolving the rest of the community and society, which produced that offender, from any sense of guilt or responsibility (Husselbee & Elliott, 2002; Meyer, 2015). This focus on pathology and personal hatred rather than on social structures and systems that uphold and maintain anti-LGBTQ laws and policies, prevents meaningful analysis and change (Gerstenfeld, 2018; Meyer, 2014, 2015). Reliance on official sources, emphasis on the offender pathology, and the focus on extreme crime events also drives public support for punitive control responses, such as sentence enhancements for hate crimes, rather than rehabilitation or treatment. Given the increasing frequency and severity of hate crimes and domestic terror incidents, it is imperative for the public to be properly informed of their causes and potential prevention. The mass shooting which occurred at the Pulse nightclub was not easily defined and was a source of national debates on terrorism, immigration, and gun control. It also spurred public discourse regarding hate crimes and the LGBTQ community.

We aimed to analyze newspaper coverage to determine how a significant mass shooting was framed and labeled, which sources were utilized to provide information, and what types of social and legal responses were offered.

Research questions

(1) What types of sources were quoted or interviewed regarding the cause of the Pulse shooting and the socio-legal response? In other words, were queer scholars, experts on hate crime, or members of the LGBTQ community relied upon, or did official criminal justice sources dominate coverage?

(a) Were official sources more or less likely than other sources to describe the shooting as a hate crime, terrorist act, or both?

(2) Which ideological frames did quoted/interviewed sources present? More specifically, was the incident discussed in regards to anti- LGBTQ discrimination, racial/ethnic prejudice, and other societal influences, or was the personal pathology of the offender emphasized?

(a) Did the ideology presented differ based upon the source's definition of the shooting as a hate crime, terrorist act, neither, or both?

Methods

We conducted content analysis of three newspapers[2] that have national scope and high readership, *The New York Times, The Washington Post*, and *USA Today*. Two of these news outlets (*The New York Times* and *The Washington Post*) are among those that serve as the 'standard bearer' or as the newspaper of record for the U.S. (see Everback, 2011; King, 1990). *USA Today* is a daily newspaper described as a populist and centrist media outlet 'aimed at a broadly based, general readership' (King, 1990, p. 84). Our focus was on the entirety of the coverage of the Pulse shooting in these nationally influential newspapers. The mass shooting was instantly a national news topic, and this study centers on the societal-level perceptions and framing of the event, thus we exclude regional and local newspapers.

Sampling

Articles were selected for analysis based on timing and content. The sample was collected by searching Lexis-Nexis with the subject term '2016 Orlando nightclub shooting' for each of the newspapers, *The New York Times, Washington Post*, and *USA Today*. Relevant news coverage of the Pulse nightclub shooting dropped substantially by the end of August, so articles were collected from the date of the shooting, 12 June 2016 through 30 August 2016. Following other studies of news media framing, we included news articles, editorials, and opinion columns (e.g. Donaldson et al., 2015). We excluded letters to the editor, obituaries, advertisements, and articles only tangentially related to the actual incident, such as entertainment articles about concerts or award ceremonies. We also eliminated duplicate articles (which was common as articles were frequently first published online and then in print edition).

Operational definitions and coding

Following Buckler, Griffin, and Travis (2008) we coded both direct (contained within quotation marks) and indirect quotes ('officials said'), for source, and crime control and crime causation ideology. Sources were coded as either Academic/Researcher, Interest Group (e.g. National Rifle Association, Human Rights Campaign), Policymaker/Politician, Official Criminal Justice Source (e.g. police, Attorney General, former FBI official), and Other (victims, bystanders, friends, family, coworkers, etc.).

We utilized the framework for evaluating news media coverage of crime causation and control ideology previously developed by Welch et al. (1998). Crime causation ideology categories include pathology, social factors, or utilitarianism. Pathology was coded as any statements attributing the cause of the shooting to the offender's mental state, personality, or perceived defect (claims regarding mental illness or impulsivity). Social factors included any statements attributing the cause of the shooting to micro- or macro-social forces, social conflicts, or social influences (for instance, anti-LGBTQ culture, anti-Muslim rhetoric, or weak gun laws). Utilitarianism was coded for statements where financial gain was described as the cause. Crime control ideology, according to Welch et al. (1998), involves support for either hard or soft control measures. Hard control includes punishment, incarceration, deterrence, and increased police powers. Soft control includes treatment, rehabilitation, criminal and social justice reform, and gun control.

While Welch, Fenwick, and Roberts (1997; 1998) established a basic structure to understand crime causation and crime control ideologies, the categories that they devised are in no way exhaustive. Situational crime prevention was popularized in the late 1970s and early 1980s (Clarke, 1980; Cohen & Felson, 1979), and serves as a viable strategy to control crime. Therefore, a third category was added as a crime control ideology, entitled 'harm mitigation,' which included preventative measures such as target-hardening, self-protection, and increased private security (Cook & Ludwig, 2011).

Both authors engaged in refining the coding framework. Only one author coded the direct and indirect quotations for the entire sample, the second analyzed a random sample of articles. Both noted any difficult or questionable quotations, discussed them, and arrived at a mutually agreeable code. It was during these meetings that the need for the third category of crime control ('harm mitigation') emerged when it became apparent that the binary option of hard versus soft control measures did not apply to some quoted statements.

Analysis

Articles were coded and analyzed by running queries in NVivo 10 for word frequency and matrix coding. Matrix coding is a cross tabulation of the coding intersections between two or more variables.

Results

A total of 232 articles were collected for analysis, nearly half (49.1%) of which were published by *The New York Times* (see Table 1). *The Washington Post* accounted for 32.3%, and 18.5% were from *USA Today*. The large difference in coverage among the papers is most likely attributable to editorial decisions about readership and newsworthiness. To provide a general overview of the focus and emphasis of the articles in the sample, a word frequency query was run to identify the top 20 most common words; the query included stemmed words and excluded words with less than four letters. After removing words that were not from the body of the articles (specifically 2016, York, Times, June, and Section), the top 20 words notably included 'Mateen,' 'Islam,' 'Terror,' and 'Muslim.' These top words strongly indicate that the dominant frame of the shooting was that of a terrorist act related to the offender's religious beliefs or influences (See Table 2).

Table 1. Sampling frame.

Newspaper	# of Articles	Word Count
The New York Times	114	113,525
The Washington Post	75	84,670
USA Today	43	22,908
Total	232	221,103

RQ 1 – Sources and descriptions

Table 3 shows the types of sources quoted in the articles and editorials about the Pulse Orlando shooting and the description or definition of the incident that they provided. We were coding for hate crime or terrorist act, but it is notable that two statements describing the incident as an act of conspiracy were also identified. Policymakers/politicians were quoted most frequently, at a rate eight times higher than that of academics/researchers and three times that of official criminal justice sources. Overall, the incident was described as a terrorist act more often than a hate crime. Policymakers/politicians and official CJ sources were more likely to call it a terrorist act than a hate crime, frequently emphasizing the role of the Islamic State or 'radical Islam':

> House Homeland Security Chairman Michael McCaul, R-Texas, said "this appears to be the worst terrorist attack on American soil since 9/11. And it is a sobering reminder that radical

Table 2. Top 20 Words.

Word	Count	Weighted Percentage (%)	Similar Words
Orlando	1273	0.91	#orlando, orlando, orlandos
People	1136	0.81	People, peoples
Mateen	1101	0.79	Mateen, mateens
Shooting	773	0.55	Shoot, shooting, shootings, shoots
Attacks	698	0.50	Attack, attacked, attacker, attackers, attacking, attacks
Islam	524	0.38	Islam, islamic, islamism
Calls	472	0.34	CALL, called, calling, calls
Kills	463	0.33	Kill, killed, killing, killings, kills
Years	459	0.33	Year, years
Trump	456	0.33	Trump, trumps
Likeness	418	0.30	Like, liked, likely, likenesses, likes
Police	414	0.30	Police, polices, policing
American	412	0.30	American, americanized, americans
Right	394	0.28	Right, rightful, rightly, rights
Nightclub	393	0.28	Nightclub, nightclubs
Communicate/ community	390	0.28	Communal, communicate, communicated, communicating, communication, communications, communicative, communities, community
Obama	389	0.28	Obama
Terror	387	0.28	Terror, terrorism, terrorize, terrorized, terrorizes
Just	384	0.28	Just, justly
Muslim	383	0.27	Muslim, muslims

Table 3. Description by source.

Description	Academic/ Researcher	Interest group	Official CJ	Others	Policymaker/ Politician	Total
Hate crime	10	11	11	25	32	89
Terrorist act	5	5	25	14	87	136
Total	15	16	36	39	119	225

> Islamists are targeting our country and our way of life," McCaul said. "But Americans will not be intimidated by these fanatics. Instead, tragedies like we saw in Orlando only strengthen our resolve to fight back against terror and prevail over extremism wherever it emerges." (*USA Today*, 13 June 2016, A3)[3]

Academics/researchers were more likely to emphasize the anti-LGBTQ nature of the attack:

> Jonathan Katz, professor of queer history at the University of Buffalo, said he noticed comments from hatemongers as well as remarks from pundits dismissing that the shooting targeted the LGBT community. "What's interesting is I often find those most interested in saying this is a crime against humanity are the same ones who are against the queer community in other contexts," he said. "If we genuinely believe that queers are part of the human community, then we can and should say this is a crime against all of us. But that entails naming, recognizing and affiliating politically and emotionally with the queer community." (*USA Today*, 20 June 2016, A8)

Leaders such as President Obama, Attorney General Loretta Lynch, and presidential candidate Hillary Clinton, labeled the attack as both a hate crime and a terrorist act. Those three individuals were quoted, in combination, a minimum of 15 times saying the exact phrase underlined here:

> "People often act out of more than one motivation," Attorney General Loretta Lynch told reporters during a visit here on Tuesday. "This was clearly an act of terror and an act of hate." (*The New York Times*, 25 June 2016, A13)

Policymakers and politicians frequently relied upon law enforcement when describing the attack, so even when recognizing that the incident targeted LGBT victims, they also clearly stated that it was being investigated as a terrorist attack. For example:

> Rep. Adam Schiff, D-Calif., the senior Democrat on the House Intelligence Committee, said he was told by police that the shooter "declared his allegiance to ISIS (the Islamic State)." "The fact that this shooting took place during Ramadan and that ISIS leadership in Raqqa has been urging attacks during this time, that the target was an LGBT night club during (LGBT) Pride (month) and, if accurate, that according to local law enforcement the shooter declared his allegiance to ISIS, indicates an ISIS-inspired act of terrorism," Schiff said. (*USA Today*, 13 June 2016, A3)

RQ 2- Ideological frames

Tables 4 and 5 provide a quantitative snapshot of causation and control ideologies by type and source. Again, policy makers/politicians were quoted more frequently than either academics/researchers or official CJ sources, but Other sources were quoted most often for causation.

Causation. Under causation there was a near even split between pathology and social factors, and no mention of utilitarianism. Official CJ sources and Other sources were most likely to attribute the cause of the shooting to the offender's pathology, while Policymakers/politicians were more likely to discuss social factors. Notably, Academics/researchers discussed both of the dominant ideologies with similar frequency. Other sources were frequently interviewed about the offender, including his father, his ex-wife, and his former coworkers and classmates. They overwhelming described him as violent, unstable, or homophobic, implying that pathology was the cause of the shooting:

Table 4. Causation by source.

Causation Ideology	Academic/ Researcher	Official CJ	Other	Policymaker/ Politician	Interest group	Total
Pathology	17	4	63	15	2	101
Social factors	17	1	29	42	9	98
Utilitarianism	0	0	0	0	0	0
Total	34	5	92	57	11	199

Table 5. Control by source.

Control Ideology	Academic/ Researcher	Official CJ	Other	Policymaker/ Politician	Interest group	Total
Hard control	3	2	2	41	2	50
Harm mitigation	0	0	2	10	7	19
Soft control	6	5	12	71	19	113
Total	9	7	16	122	28	182

> But there also were early signs of emotional trouble and a volatile temper, according to Sitora Yusifiy, who was briefly married to Mateen. Yusifiy described Mateen as an abusive husband who beat her repeatedly while they were married. "He was not a stable person," ... "He beat me. He would just come home and start beating me up because the laundry wasn't finished or something like that." (*The Washington Post*, 13 June 2016, A1)

> Daniel Gilroy ... said Mateen frequently made homophobic and racial comments. Gilroy said he complained to G4S several times, but said the employer did nothing. Gilroy quit after he said Mateen began stalking him via text messages – 20 or 30 a day, he said. Mateen also sent Gilroy 13 to 15 phone messages daily. "This guy was unhinged and unstable," said Gilroy. "He talked of killing people." (*USA Today*, 13 June 2016, A1)

Much of the discussion involved questions or assumptions about the offender's sexual orientation and his homophobic attitudes:

> Seddique Mateen said he didn't believe his son was gay, telling reporters, "I don't believe he was a whatever-you-call-it." He said his son Mateen had become enraged a few months earlier at the sight of a pair of gay men being affectionate with each other. "We were in downtown Miami, Bayside, people were playing music. And he saw two men kissing each other in front of his wife and kid and he got very angry," he told reporters. "They were kissing each other and touching each other and he said: 'Look at that. In front of my son they are doing that." (*The Washington Post*, 13 June 2016, A1)

Policy makers and politicians frequently discussed social and political issues such as immigration, religion, anti-LGBTQ policies, and lax gun control laws, as causes of the shooting. Here are examples:

> He blamed the Orlando attack – which authorities say was carried out by a man born in America to Afghan parents – in part on a system that "allowed his family to come here." "Once again we've seen that political correctness is deadly," Trump said. "And just so you understand: I have many Muslim friends," he added at one point. "There doesn't seem to be assimilation. We don't know what's going on." (*The Washington Post*, 15 June 2016, A1)

> "If one more Republican tells me they have gay friends, I'm gonna scream," said Representative Sean Patrick Maloney, Democrat of New York and one of just a few openly gay, lesbian or bisexual members of Congress. "I don't care that they have gay friends. I care that they're voting against equality." (*The New York Times*, 16 June 2016, A17)

> I freely admit that I identified entirely with Sen. Chris Murphy (D-Conn.) when he declared: "This phenomenon of near constant mass shootings happens only in America – nowhere else. Congress has become complicit in these murders by its total, unconscionable deafening silence." (*The Washington Post*, 13 June 2016, A21)

Control. Across the board, all source types advocated for soft control measures and/or criticized hard control measures as the appropriate socio-legal response to the Pulse Orlando shooting. Politicians/policymakers, who also discussed harm mitigation and hard control measures, were quoted the most on the subject. Gun control laws were a major topic of discussion in the aftermath of the shooting and account for most of the discussion of soft control measures:

> The president said he hoped lawmakers who blocked his 2013 gun-control push after the shooting deaths of 20 first-graders in Newtown, Conn., would have a change of heart. And he declared that "the notion that the answer to this tragedy would be to make sure that more people in a nightclub are similarly armed to the killer defies common sense." (*The Washington Post*, 17 June 2016, A6)

> "We passed gun control in this state," said Mr. Cuomo, a Democrat, standing before a lectern festooned with a sign declaring "We Are Orlando," and flanked by an American flag and a gay pride flag. "We outlawed assault weapons in this state. We know it can be done." He added, "Until we have a national policy, none of us are safe." (*The New York Times*, 14 June 2016, A14)

Policymakers and politicians across the political spectrum criticized (then presidential candidate) Trump's calls for a ban on Muslim immigration:

> Rep. Adam Kinzinger (R-Ill.), an Air Force veteran who flew missions in Iraq and Afghanistan, said it would be detrimental to demonize an entire religion as Trump is doing. "To just simply say ban them all – I think frankly does more harm," Kinzinger said ... "It may work for a political season and it does, maybe it's a popular sound bite, but it is very detrimental to our long-term ability to actually win this war." (*The Washington Post*, 14 June 2016, A1)

> "A ban on Muslims would not have stopped this attack. Neither would a wall. I don't know how one builds a wall to keep the Internet out," Clinton said. "Not one of Donald Trump's reckless ideas would have saved a single life in Orlando." (*The Washington Post*, 16 June 2016, A6)

President Obama, as well as academics/researchers, noted the complexity and the challenge of addressing multiple causes, such as gun availability and extremist ideology. These are examples from the news items:

> "My concern," Obama said, "is that we start getting into a debate, as has happened in the past, which is an either/or debate, and the suggestion is either we think about something as terrorism and we ignore the problems with easy access to firearms. Or it's all about firearms and we ignore the role, the very real role, that organizations like [the Islamic State] have in generating extremist views inside this country. It's not an either/or. It's a both/and." (*The Washington Post*, 14 June 2016, A10)

> Mr. Clarke says the United States needs to institute a "much more thorough program" to counter that propaganda. He also says that preventing terrorism suspects from having easy access to lethal weapons should be a no-brainer. But he warns that there are no panaceas. "When a guy one minute suggests he may be sympathetic to ISIS and the next minute

> decides to kill people, catching that minute is really, really hard," he says. (*The New York Times*, 20 June 2016)

Official CJ sources also promoted soft control measures. The following is a quote that seemingly advocates for prevention efforts:

> "Tools other than arrest and prosecution need to be established," said George Selim, who leads the administration's Countering Violent Extremism Task Force from DHS. (*The Washington Post*, 5 July 2016, A1)

When interest groups promoted soft control measures, they discussed education, training, and tolerance. For instance:

> Haiman-Marrero said local leaders were planning an event to demonstrate solidarity between central Florida's Latino and Muslim communities. The fact that the killer was a Muslim and that most of his victims were Latino, she said, should not cause a rift between the two cultures. "We're not pointing fingers. We can't point fingers. This needs to stop," Haiman-Marrero said. "I could not care less what Trump has to say. We are stopping the cycle of intolerance. "We will not judge the character of a community based on the actions of one individual." (*The Washington Post*, 14 June 2016, A14)

Policymakers/politicians also provided support for hard control measures such as expanding police power and taking military action:

> Mr. Trump ... said in particular that he would ban immigration from countries where terrorism was a threat. He said, referring to the assailant in Orlando, that "thousands and thousands of people, many of whom have the same thought process as this savage killer" are pouring into the country, and that the ban "will be lifted when and as a nation we are in a position to properly and perfectly screen these people coming into our country." (*The New York Times*, 13 June 2016)

> Hillary Clinton, the presumptive Democratic nominee, released a statement saying: "We need to redouble our efforts to defend our country from threats at home and abroad. That means defeating international terror groups, working with allies and partners to go after them wherever they are, countering their attempts to recruit people here and everywhere, and hardening our defenses at home." (*The New York Times*, 13 June 2016)

Harm mitigation was not a common ideology, but interest groups, politicians, and others promoted it:

> On Wednesday, Donald Trump took time out from vilifying Muslims and put some of the blame on gun control. If the patrons of Pulse, the gay bar in Orlando, had been carrying concealed weapons, he said, they could have taken control of the situation. The gunman would have been "just open target practice." (*The New York Times*, 16 June 2016, A23)

> When I reached Isquith on his cellphone, on the convention floor, he said that for furniture makers, "security is the big new frontier, if you will. It's kind of sad to say that, but it's true." In a news release that morning, he noted that the kind of "violence and terror" seen in Orlando was "not going away anytime soon." His product, the release said, offered "a 21st-century solution to saving lives and reducing injuries to innocent people in public spaces during an active-shooter event." (*The New York Times Magazine*, 25 June 2016, p.15)

RQ 2 – Description and framing

Soft control measures were the dominant control ideology, regardless of whether the act was described as a terrorist attack, hate crime, both, or neither. Examples include:

> Democrats, led by Sen. Dianne Feinstein of California, are pushing to give the attorney general authority to bar gun sales to suspected terrorists, under many of the same criteria used to put people on the nation's no-fly and other broad terrorism watchlists. "If you're too dangerous to get on a plane," presumptive Democratic presidential nominee Hillary Clinton said last week, "you're too dangerous to buy a gun." (*USA Today*, 20 June 2016, A8)

> House Speaker Paul D. Ryan (Wis.) denounced Trump for trying to rally support for his anti-Muslim policies, while others castigated Trump for the accusations he has lobbed at Obama. "I do not think a Muslim ban is in our country's interest," Ryan told reporters. "I do not think it is reflective of our principles, not just as a party but as a country." (*The Washington Post*, 15 June 2016, A1)

In fact, when discussing control measures, quoted sources tended to emphasize the availability of guns, and did not frame the attack as either a hate crime or a terrorist act. For instance:

> "Those who were killed and injured here were gunned down by a single killer with a powerful assault weapon," Obama said. "The motives of this killer may have been different than the mass killers in Aurora, or Newtown. But the instruments of death were so similar. Now another 49 innocent people are dead. Another 53 are injured. Some are still fighting for their lives. Some will have wounds that will last a lifetime." Obama tried to acknowledge the complex mix of motivations and causes of the Orlando attack, but focused mostly on just one: guns. (*USA Today*, 17 June 2016, A3)

When hard control measures were promoted, however, such as the expansion of police and military powers through immigration bans or surveillance of Muslim Americans, it was always tied to a terrorism framing of the incident:

> In his speech Monday ... Trump appeared to expand his policy. If elected, he said, he would "suspend immigration from areas of the world where there's a proven history of terrorism against the United States, Europe or our allies until we fully understand how to end these threats." (*The Washington Post*, 14 June 2016, A1)

> But this week Gov. Rick Scott, a Republican, stressed that it was radical Islam that needed to be controlled, not guns. "The Second Amendment didn't kill anybody," Mr. Scott said. "Evil, radical Islam, ISIS – they killed." (*The New York Times*, 16 June 2016, A1)

Summary

The national newspapers analyzed in this study relied far more heavily on official sources, in the form of policy makers and politicians, than on criminal justice sources, academics/researchers, or any other source. Those policymakers/politicians framed the shooting primarily as an act of terror and promoted soft control measures, in the form of gun control laws, and criticized presidential candidate Trump's hard control ideology. The role of criminal justice officials is blurred. They were quoted far more often than is reflected in this analysis because they spoke primarily in order to present factual information about an ongoing investigation, and rarely presented ideological frames. Policymakers and politicians, however, relied heavily upon that investigative role and frequently referred directly to the information given by police or the FBI, which likely impacted framing and resulted in terrorism as the dominant description of the shooting.

Discussion

Reliance on official sources over academics was expected, though perhaps discouraging, and aligns with the earlier work by Buckler et al. (2008). The dominant frame of a pathological offender committing a terrorist act was also expected, and can be mostly attributed to the media's habit of personalizing offenders by interviewing known associates. The media attempt to create personal profiles of terrorists that focus on 'exposing the tragedy of an individual,' rather than providing a neutral presentation of the incident and its socio-political ramifications (Kampf, 2014, p. 5). This study and prior work suggests that perhaps academics and researchers could act as a counter balance. Whereas politicians and practitioners' quotes typically focus more on crime control, professors and researchers address crime causation, and can counterbalance politicians and practitioners by focusing attention on social factors (Welch et al., 1998).

The dominance of soft control measures as preferred socio-legal response was surprising, particularly since it was even found in combination with terrorist framing or descriptions. Previous research found that hard control measures were the dominant ideology of politicians and practitioners when discussing crime (Welch et al., 1998). This unexpected finding may be attributed to one or more contextual factors. Criminal justice is often a bipartisan policy arena and reform has been a priority that spans the political spectrum for much of the 21st century (Levin, 2019; Levin, 2018). The Pulse attack occurred during a democratic Presidential administration that actively promoted soft control measures like gun control and prison and sentencing reform (Lartey, 2016). Additionally, hate crime scholars have frequently advocated for soft control measures, such as anti-bias education, and criticized the punitive sentence enhancements given to hate crime offenders because longer prison sentences cannot treat or solve prejudice and bigotry (Gerstenfeld, 2018; Meyer, 2014; Mogul, Ritchie, & Whitlock, 2011). So, the dominance of soft control measures may also be a reflection of contemporary scholarly thinking around issues of bias and prejudice, even though academics/researchers were rarely utilized as sources by reporters.

In the coverage of the Pulse attack there was a noticeable lack of attention to victims and the potential that their perception of the attack was an anti-LGBTQ hate crime committed against an almost entirely Latinx population. A large portion of quoted sources were categorized as 'other,' but most of those sources were associates of the offender. Victims and their friends and family received considerably less attention and were quoted rarely. In cases of mass shooting, news media organizations seem to place considerable attention on understanding the cause and motives of the offender. This necessitates an investigation into the life of the offender and leads journalists to sources of information that were close in spatial or emotional proximity to the offender. Moreover, the direction of the commentary from key government and political sources was that the event was motivated by terrorist ideology rather than personal prejudice, and this likely impacted the narrative that media organizations pursued.

Only a few statements made by quoted sources contextualized the anti-LGBTQ nature of the attack within the social and political climate that harms and discriminates against the LGBTQ community. Most of the discussion of the offender's potential bias against his victims was described as an individual failing; his homophobia was framed as pathology. Ott and Aoki (2002) also found this to be the case in their media analysis of Matthew Shepard's murder in which coverage actually shifted from recognition of the social context to complete focus on homophobia as a character flaw of the offenders. Scholars have heavily criticized this view of homophobia, as solely an individual trait disconnected from the environment that created it (Herek, 2015; Worthen, 2014), because both social and political hostility toward LGBTQ people remains strong. Conversion therapy is legally practiced in many states, despite knowledge of its harms, housing and employment discrimination is legal, religious refusal laws are being pushed in several states, and the current Trump administration has worked to reverse or repeal numerous policies that recognized LGBTQ Americans (National Center for Transgender Equality, 2019). The term homophobia implies that prejudice against sexual minorities is a personal, debilitating fear requiring treatment, but homophobic people do not want to be cured, and do not express fear, rather anger and hostility (Herek, 2015). Sexual stigma (and cisgenderism), however, is embedded within law, policy, institutions, media, language, and pretty much of every other part of human culture (Herek, 2015), and influences the behavior and experiences of both heterosexual and non-heterosexual individuals (Worthen, 2014).

It is, however, notable that some leading political figures quoted by news media sought to define the event as an act of terror and as an act of hate. This event – perhaps more so than any other mass killing event in the history of the United States – points to the complexity inherent in attempts to label this sort of act as either one or the other. While there is ample evidence that United States foreign policy and actions spurred the thinking of the offender, it is an inescapable fact that the aggression was levied not at white, heterosexual persons (the dominant social group in the U.S.), but, rather, at a marginalized population with respect to both sexual orientation and ethnicity. This makes the attack appear to be a 'downward crime,' as hate crimes typically are (Deloughery et al., 2012). The victims of the attack were almost entirely minorities, many of them holding intersecting minority statuses as both LGBTQ and Latinx. The fact that so many of them were specifically Puerto Rican is important because they came to Orlando in order to escape poverty and find opportunities unavailable to them on an island decimated by colonial neglect (Sullivan & Hernandez, 2016). But far more attention was given to the offender's minority status as the Muslim son of Afghan immigrants who had a long history of being bullied and acting violently and disruptively. The nuance of a minority-on-minority hate crime was lost as politicians and commentators raced to label the attack as a terrorist act against 'all of us.' A significant number of hate crimes are committed between two minority groups as they struggle to move up a rung on the social ladder (Gerstenfeld, 2018). Minority groups are strongly influenced by the dominant culture and may choose the same victims and scapegoats of white masculine supremacy (Perry, 2001). Regardless of the conclusions of the FBI investigation on the matter, there is a strong undercurrent to this event which implies that it cannot be understood singularly as an act of terror or as an act of hatred because of the marginality of both the victims and the offender.

The consequences of the one or the other terrorism-hatred dichotomy that played out politically and in the news media are not readily apparent, but they exist. When political leaders squabble over whether events like this should be classified as an act of terror or as an act of hatred, it further exacerbates social divisions that are rooted not only in race, ethnicity, gender, gender identity, and sexual orientation, but also in society's general acceptance of difference and diversity. As Jacobs and Potter (1998) argued, hate crime laws are often merely symbolic and can actually work to increase, rather than decrease, social conflict. In this instance, the law recognizes the necessity to punish more stringently an offender who targets a large number of people from a socially marginalized population (see United States Sentencing Commission, 2019). If Omar Mateen had been taken into police custody alive and convicted, he likely would have faced an upward sentence for committing an offense against vulnerable victims and for the number of victims. While the law recognizes the difficulty of separating the primary motive (terrorism) from the outcome of the act (a number of deaths of a vulnerable population), this basic fact never made it into the mainstream discussions of the legal and social implications of this case.

Policy implications

Gun control came up as both a causation and control issue. When guns are blamed for crime, it is discussed as a social factor necessitating socio-legal responses. Firearms of all kinds are easily purchased in a variety of manners in the United States and, increasingly, can be openly carried in public spaces. It was easy to code pro-gun control arguments as soft control for this analysis because it was explicitly listed as such by Welch et al. (1998). Gun control and gun safety legislation has become a partisan issue, but when terrorism is the cause, both sides, and even interest groups like the NRA, tend to agree that government should use its power to regulate and control the sale and purchase of firearms to potential terrorists. If framed as an expansion of police power, then, it could be viewed as a hard control issue, rather than a soft one. Regardless, gun violence continues to be a serious social problem which the federal government appears unwilling to address.

It is common for public support for victims of hate crimes to spike following a publicized incident (see Husselbee & Elliott, 2002; Ott & Aoki, 2002), but it does not necessarily lead to policy change. Matthew Shepard and James Byrd, Jr. were memorialized in the name of the federal Hate Crimes Protection Act of 2009, which passed over a decade after their murders, but the state of Wyoming, where Shepard was killed, has yet to pass a single hate crime law. Since the Pulse shooting, the state of Florida has not taken any steps to improve hate crime protections and the state law still fails to cover gender or gender identity (Santich, 2019). Gun control legislation, or the lack thereof, was attributed as both a cause of the Pulse shooting, and urged as a necessary control response (as is commonly the case following a public mass shooting). Yet, neither the state of Florida nor the federal government has passed a single piece of legislation aimed at reducing the availability of firearms or increasing gun safety. The noticeable lack of attention to victim perceptions and minimal quoting of academics and criminal justice experts could potentially explain why media attention is insufficient for policy change.

Limitations & future research

Some studies of news media framing have begun to include both television and print news in their analyses as a way to counter concerns regarding decreased readership (e.g. Donaldson et al., 2015), but including television news was simply outside the scope of this article. Future research should also examine national television news coverage. Additionally, this study is limited to three national newspapers of record, therefore, the results may not be generalizable to other newspapers throughout the nation that covered the event. We did not focus attention on more regionally-known newspapers such as the *Atlanta Constitution, Boston Globe*, or *Chicago Tribune*, or on local papers like the *Orlando Sentinel* due to our concern with the national discourse and societal-level understanding of the event. This is understandably a limitation of the study. The Pulse shooting may have been presented and framed differentially across local and regional newspapers based on the social and political culture of the news outlet and the region. Future research could also further examine the portrayal of the victims or use mixed methods to analyze the impact of the event and the coverage upon public opinion and legislation.

Conclusion

News media coverage of crime has the potential to incite fear and fuel emotional outrage, and is an important influence on public opinions of crime and the criminal justice system. This study shows that news reporters continue to rely on official sources, especially politicians, and that offender pathology continues to be blamed for violent crimes. Soft control measures are now widely-discussed and offered as appropriate response and prevention tactics, even in cases of terrorism, though federal legislation has not followed this change in public discourse. This study also confirms that national concerns and federal resources are centered on terrorism and perceived pathological offenders which prevents adequate recognition and attention to sociological factors and significant harms caused to victims and their communities. For the LGBTQ and Latinx communities, this study confirms their observations and feelings of neglect in the aftermath of the Pulse shooting, as the majority of sources in the national newspapers focused on the offender and his pathology and ideology, while those most able to discuss the cause and impact of such a crime against the LGBTQ and Latinx communities were rarely quoted. As Jonathan Katz, the sole queer scholar to be quoted, observed, dismissing the fact that the queer Latinx community was the target of the attack, and not the general public, strongly suggests that many in society are still unable to associate and empathize with the queer community (Solis, 2016).

Notes

1. The Hate Crime Statistics Act, 28 U.S.C. § 534 (2010).
2. It is recognized that since 1990 the circulation of newspapers in the U.S. has precipitously declined (see Pew Research Center's 'Newspapers Fact Sheet' from 9 July 2019, https://www.journalism.org/fact-sheet/newspapers/). However, according to the work of Protess and McCombs (1991), television news is directly influenced by coverage in newspapers. Our decision to focus on national newspapers rather than national television news programs was influenced by a desire to understand the breadth of coverage of the event. With respect to what is covered and how extensively it is covered by

national newspapers is influenced by column inches, whereas national television news programs generally run for 30 minutes a day. A newspaper has more capacity than televised news programs to cover more relevant topics in a news event and to cover them for longer periods of time as more information becomes known about the event.
3. The citation method used here follows that used in other content analyses of news media, e.g. Welch et al. (1998).

Disclosure statement

No potential conflict of interest was reported by the authors.

References

Beydoun, K.A. (2018). Lone wolf terrorism: Types, stripes, and double-standards. *Northwestern University Law Review, 112*(5), 1213–1243.

Bjelopera, J.P. (2016). Sifting domestic terrorism from hate crime and homegrown violent extremism (IN10299). Congressional Research Service Insight.

Black, D. (2004). Terrorism as social control. *Sociology of Crime, Law and Deviance, 5*, 9–18.

Brinson, M., & Stohl, M. (2009). From 7/7 to 8/10: Media framing of terrorist incidents in the United States and United Kingdom. *The Faces of Terrorism... Multidisciplinary Perspectives*, 227–244.

Buckler, K., Griffin, T., & Travis, L.F., III. (2008). Criminologists as "benchwarmers:" The exclusion of eggheads from crime news discourse. *Southwest Journal of Criminal Justice, 5*(1), 4–21.

Buist, C.L., & Lenning, E. (2016). *Queer criminology*. New York, NY: Routledge.

Chagnon, N. (2015). Reverberate, resonate, reproduce: A reconsideration of ideological influence in crime news production. *Critical Criminology, 23*(1), 105–123.

Clark, S. (2019). Confronting the domestic right-wing terrorist threat. Center for American Progress. Retrieved from https://cdn.americanprogress.org/content/uploads/2019/03/06082055/Right-WingTerrorism-brief.pdf.

Clarke, R. (1980). "Situational" crime prevention: Theory and practice. *British Journal of Criminology, 20*(2), 136–147.

Cohen, L., & Felson, M. (1979). Social change and crime rate trends: A routine activity approach. *American Sociological Review, 44*(4), 588–608.

Cook, P.J., & Ludwig, J. (2011). The economist's guide to crime busting. *The Wilson Quarterly, 35*(1), 62–66.

Dastiger, A.E. (2017, June 12). 2016 was the deadliest year on record for the LGBTQ community. *USA Today*. Retrieved from https://www.usatoday.com/story/news/nation/2017/06/12/2016deadliest-year-lgbtq-pulse/373840001/

Deloughery, K., King, R.D., & Asal, V. (2012). Close cousins or distant relatives? The relationship between terrorism and hate crime. *Crime & Delinquency, 58*(5), 663–688.

Donaldson, E.A., Cohen, J.E., Truant, P.L., Rutkow, L., Kanarek, N.F., & Berry, C.L. (2015). News media framing of New York City's sugar-sweetened beverage portion-size cap. *American Journal of Public Health, 105*(11), 2202–2209.

Duwe, G. (2007). *Mass murder in the United States: A history*. Jefferson, NC: McFarland & Company, Inc.

Everback, T. (2011). A "wise Latina" and a son of immigrants: Comparing newspaper coverage of Sonia Sotomayor and Samuel Alito. *Southwestern Mass Communication Journal, 26*, 1–14.
FBI. (2018). Crime in the United States 2018. Retrieved from https://ucr.fbi.gov/crime-in-the-u.s/2018/crime-in-the-u.s.-2018
FBI. (2019). Terrorism. Retrieved from https://www.fbi.gov/investigate/terrorism
Ferguson, R.A. (2018). The Pulse nightclub and the state of our world. *GLQ: A Journal of Lesbian and Gay Studies, 24*(1), 36–38.
Gerstenfeld, P.B. (2018). *Hate crimes: Causes, controls, and controversies* (*4th* ed.). Washington, DC: Sage.
Halzak, S., Hui, M., & O'Connell, J. (2016, June 14). Venues and festivals across the country take a closer look at safety measures. *The Washington Post*, p. A17.
Hauser, C., & Blinder, A. (2016, September 13). Arson is suspected at mosque that Orlando nightclub gunman attended. *The New York Times*, p. A17.
Hauslohner, A., Achenbach, J., & Nakashima, E. (2016, September 24). They're the same people. *Washington Post*, p. A1.
Herek, G.M. (2015). Beyond "homophobia": Thinking more clearly about stigma, prejudice, and sexual orientation. *American Journal of Orthopsychiatry, 85*(5), S29–S37.
Hodges, R., & Sommerstein, A. (2018). 42 law enforcement officers murdered by domestic extremists since 2005. Southern Poverty Law Center. Retrieved from: https://www.splcenter.org/20180927/42-law-enforcement-officers-murdered-domesticextremists-2005
Husselbee, L.P., & Elliott, L. (2002). Looking beyond hate: How national and regional newspapers framed hate crimes in Jasper, Texas, and Laramie, Wyoming. *Journalism and Mass Communication Quarterly, 79*(4), 833–852.
Jacobs, J.B., & Potter, K. (1998). *Hate crimes: Criminal law and identity politics*. New York: Oxford University Press.
Jones, S.G. (2018). The rise of far-right extremism in the United States. Center for Strategic and International Studies. Research Brief. Retrieved from www.csis.org.
Kampf, Z. (2014). News-media and terrorism: Changing relationship, changing definitions. *Sociology Compass, 8*(1), 1–9.
Kearns, E.M., Betus, A.E., & Lemieux, A.F. (2019). Why do some terrorist attacks receive more media attention than others? *Justice Quarterly, 36*(6), 985–1022.
King, E.G. (1990). Thematic coverage of the 1988 presidential primaries: A comparison of USA today and the New York Times. *Journalism Quarterly, 67*(1), 83–87.
Krouse, W.J., & Richardson, D.J. (2015). Mass murder with firearms: Incidents and victims, 1999-2013. *Congressional Research Service, 7-5700*, R44126.
La Fountain-Stokes, L. (2018). Nunca olvidar/to never forget: Pulse Orlando. *GLQ: A Journal of Lesbian and Gay Studies, 24*(1), 17–26.
Lantz, B., & Kim, J. (2019). Hate crimes hurt more, but so do co-offenders: Separating the influence of co-offending and bias on hate-motivated physical injury. *Criminal Justice & Behavior, 46*(3), 437–456.
Lartey, J. (2016). Obama made progress on criminal justice reform. Will it survive the next president? *The Guardian*. Retrieved from https://www.theguardian.com/us-news/2016/nov/14/barack-obamacriminal-justice-reform-prison-sentencing-police.
Lawrence, F.M. (2016, June 15). *Why calling the Orlando shooting a hate crime matters: Analysis*. Retrieved from http://www.msnbc.com/msnbc/mass-shooting-orlando-represents-both-terrorism-and-hate-crime-analysis
Levin, B. (2019). The consensus myth in criminal justice reform. *Michigan Law Review, 117*(2), 259–318.
Levin, M. (2018). Finding smart ways to be tough on crime: A perspective on federal criminal justice reform. *Texas Review of Law & Politics, 23*(2), 327–334.
Lewis, C.S. (2014). *Tough on hate?: The cultural politics of hate crimes*. Rutgers University Press.
Mabon, S., & Royle, S. (2016). *The origins of ISIS: The collapse of nations and revolution in the Middle East*. Bloomsbury Publishing.
McDevitt, J., Levin, J., & Bennett, S. (2002). Hate crime offenders: An expanded typology. *Journal of Social Issues, 58*(2), 303–317.
Meyer, D. (2014). Resisting hate crime discourse: Queer and intersectional challenges to neoliberal hate crime laws. *Critical Criminology, 22*(1), 113–125.

Meyer, D. (2015). *Violence against queer people: Race, class, gender, and the persistence of anti-LGBT discrimination*. New Brunswick, New Jersey: Rutgers University Press.

Mogul, J.L., Ritchie, A.J., & Whitlock, K. (2011). *Queer (In)justice: The criminalization of LGBT people in the United States*. Beacon Press.

Montero, D. (2019). Police release more documents connected to Las Vegas mass shooting. *Los Angeles Times*. Retrieved from https://www.latimes.com/nation/la-na-vegas-shooting-videos-20190320story.html.

National Center for Transgender Equality. (2019). The discrimination administration. https://transequality.org/the-discrimination-administration

National Consortium for the Study of Terrorism and Responses to Terrorism. (2016). Extreme hatred: Revisiting the hate crime and terrorism relationship. START Research Brief. Retrieved from www.start.umd.edu.

Norris, J.J. (2017). Why Dylann Roof is a terrorist under federal law, and why it matters. *Harv. J. on Legis., 54*, 259.

Ott, B.L., & Aoki, E. (2002). The politics of negotiating public tragedy: Media framing of the Matthew Shepard murder. *Rhetoric & Public Affairs, 5*(3), 483–505.

Perry, B. (2001). *In the name of hate: Understanding hate crimes*. Psychology Press.

Potter, G.W., & Kappeler, V.E. (2006). *Constructing crime: Perspectives on making news and social problems*. Long Grove, IL: Waveland Press.

Powell, K.A. (2011). Framing Islam: An analysis of U.S. media coverage of terrorism since 9/11. *Communication Studies, 62*(1), 90–112.

Ritchie, H. (2019, May 29). Does the news reflect what we die from? *Our World in Data*. Retrieved from https://ourworldindata.org/does-the-news-reflect-what-we-die-from.

Santich, K. (2019, April 12). Florida's hate crime law marred by holes, advocates say. *Orlando Sentinel*. Retrieved from https://www.orlandosentinel.com/news/os-ne-florida-hate-crime law-20190412-story.html

Solis, S. (2016, June 20). ISIL or not, shooting was hate crime against LGBT people. *USA Today*, News, p. 8A.

St. George, D. (2016, June 15). Muslim students report bias amid terror wave. *The Washington Post*, p. B1.

Sullivan, K., & Hernandez, A. (2016, June 14). Latino community hit hard. *The Washington Post*, p. A1.

Tillery, B., Ray, A., Cruz, E., & Waters, E. (2018). Lesbian, gay, bisexual, transgender, queer and HIV-affected hate and intimate partner violence in 2017. *National Coalition of Anti-Violence Programs*. Retrieved from www.ncavp.org.

United States Sentencing Commission. (2019). *Federal sentencing guidelines manual*. St. Paul, MN: West Publishing Co.

Valcore, J.L., & Dodge, M. (2019). How hate crime legislation shapes gay and lesbian target groups: An analysis of social construction, law, and policy. *Criminal Justice Policy Review, 30* (2), 293–315.

Waters, E., Jindasurat, C., & Wolfe, C. (2016). Lesbian, gay, bisexual, transgender, queer, and HIV-affected hate violence in 2015. New York, NY: National Coalition of Anti-Violence Programs (NCAVP).

Welch, M., Fenwick, M., & Roberts, M. (1997). Primary definitions of crime and moral panic: A content analysis of experts' quotes in feature newspaper articles on crime. *Journal of Research in Crime and Delinquency, 34*(4), 474–494.

Welch, M., Fenwick, M., & Roberts, M. (1998). State managers, intellectuals, and the media: A content analysis of ideology in experts' quotes in feature newspaper articles on crime. *Justice Quarterly, 15* (2), 219–241.

Worthen, M.G.F. (2014). The cultural significance of homophobia on heterosexual women's gendered experiences in the United States: A commentary. *Sex Roles, 71*(3–4), 141–151.

What staff need to know: using elements of gender-responsive programming to create safer environments for system-involved LGBTQ girls and women

Lindsay Kahle Semprevivo and Jill Leslie Rosenbaum

ABSTRACT

Lesbian, gay, bisexual, transgender, queer and/or questioning (LGBTQ) youth and adults are disproportionately in contact with the juvenile and criminal justice systems. Despite disproportionate representation, the system is ill-equipped to attend to the needs of these populations. While one of the greatest contributions of feminist criminology was gender-responsive programming, assuming that all girls and women share the same struggles and needs renders non-heterosexual and non-gender binary identities invisible. The purpose of this article is to focus on training staff in two primary elements of gender-responsive programming, *developing cultural appropriateness* and *competence*, and *responses to sexism and homophobia*, in order to provide safer environments for system-involved LGBTQ girls and women.

Over the past several decades, feminist criminology has pioneered a change in theory and practice, and how criminology can adequately focus on and address the needs of women and minorities. Gender-responsive programming (GRP) is one of many important contributions, and has been particularly useful in helping girls and women in the criminal justice system. According to Bloom and Covington, gender responsiveness consistently acknowledges, 'the realities of women's lives, including the pathways they travel to criminal offending and the relationships that shape their lives' (Bloom, Owen, & Covington, 2003, p. 75). It is important to remember, however, that all girls and women are not the same. As Bloom, Owen, and Covington outline, there are vast differences in women across class membership, age, race and ethnicity, as well as sexual orientation. Gender-responsive programming highlights that such differences must be a centralized focus when providing policies and programs that concentrate on the needs of women. By using and expanding the framework of GRP, the purpose of this paper is to emphasize the differences in the needs of (and training of staff in contact with) system-involved girls and women who identify as members of the lesbian, gay, bisexual, transgender, queer and/or questioning (LGBTQ) community.

Embedded throughout the principles of gender-responsive programming is the need for all services to be trauma informed. Covington and Bloom (2000) argue that services for women must take trauma into account, avoid triggering trauma reactions, avoid retraumatizing individuals, and ensure staff have a full understanding of the individual's coping. Truama informed care must also be used when working with LGBTQ identified folks because there is an overwhelming amount of evidence that sexual orientation and non-binary gender identity also shapes trajectories for involvement in the criminal justice system. Research by the Resource Center for Mental Health Promotion and Youth Violence Prevention discussed how LGBTQ youth face traumatic experiences (i.e. bullying, harassment, victimization, stigma, discrimination, isolation ... etc.) in their everyday lives, and that such events can have overwhelming consequences for them (Adopting a trauma-informed approach for LGBTQ youth, n.d.). For example, LGBTQ youth and adults are disproportionately at risk for all types of victimization (Dank, Lachman, Zweig, & Yahner, 2014; Freedner, Freed, Yang, & Austin, 2002; Kann et al., 2014), they are over twice as likely to have experienced homelessness, family conflict, and child abuse (Hunt & Moodie-Mills, 2012), and even experience disproportionate sentencing (Valentino, 2011), and utter invisibility by the juvenile justice system. (Irvine, 2010; Quinn, Poirier, & Garfinkel, 2005). Research also finds that issues of violence and victimization are unfortunately exacerbated by institutional levels of discrimination, such as heterosexism, homophobia, biphobia, and transphobia (Herek, 1990), as well as discrimination, internalizing discriminatory attitudes, a person's degree of outness, dependency, jealousy, and power imbalances between partners (Messinger, 2017; Renzetti, 1992).

There are a significant number of system-involved girls and women who identify as members of the LGBTQ community. In comparison to the broader population, LGBTQ youth and adults are overrepresented in the criminal and juvenile justice systems. For example, Marksamer and Tobin (2014) outline that, in comparison to 2.7% of adults, 16% of transgender adults have gone to prison or jail at some point in their lives. Other studies find that anywhere from 13% to 20% of youth in detention facilities identify as LGBT (Irvine, 2010; Irvine & Canfield, 2017; Irvine, Wilber, & Canfield, 2017), and there is a significant cross-over between LGBTQ youth in the child welfare system and the juvenile justice system (Irvine, 2016). Furthermore, research by Himmelstein and Bruckner (2011) found that LGBTQ girls were more likely to be suspended, expelled, detained, arrested, and incarcerated for exhibiting similar behaviors as their heteronormative peers.

Unfortunately, despite overrepresentation in the criminal justice system, it significantly lacks the necessary tools for addressing the needs of LGBTQ offenders. Research finds that LGBTQ youth in the system face many obstacles, including significant safety issues (including harassment by peers and staff once in the system), a lack of visibility, a lack of training and knowledge about LGBTQ issues among staff, a lack of policies and services that protect LGBTQ youth, and even a lack of appropriate sentencing options for LGBTQ youth (Feinstein, Greenblatt, Hass, Kohn, & Rana, 2001). Perhaps the greatest irony here is that LGBTQ youth desire resources that can improve their situation. According to Belknap, Holsinger, and Little (2014), sexual minority status (SMS) youth in delinquent facilities desired more treatment and counseling than their non-SMS counterparts. More specifically, SMS youth significantly desired more services that addressed sexual abuse, physical abuse, family counseling, individual counseling, and depression (or other mental health) counseling services. However, after experiencing providers' discriminative attitudes and biases, lesbian patients were less likely to seek the help they desired. Given these findings, the need to adapt gender-responsive programs to be more attuned to the needs of LGBTQ girls and women is crucial.

In order to provide trauma-informed care for women and girls (especially those who identify as members of the LGBTQ community), staff must first be aware of what trauma is, what kinds of things cause traumatization, and how to recognize and respond to trauma-related behavior. Our former work (Kahle & Rosenbaum, 2019)) expanded the basic principles of gender-responsive programming to include LGBTQ girls and women (see below), and our purpose here is to focus precisely on preparing staff to work with justice-involved LGBTQ girls and women by expanding on two primary principles, 1) *developing cultural appropriateness* and *competence*, and 2) *responses to sexism and homophobia*. Overall, this paper uses multiple interdisciplinary recommendations and examples to show how staff must be trained in cultural appropriateness and competence, as well as how to appropriately deal with and respond to sexism and homophobia when working with justice-involved LGBTQ girls and women.

Recognizing the Need for LGBTQ-Specific Training and Programming

There are a number of studies that have identified the major challenges faced when implementing gender-responsive programs in correctional facilities, the most prominent being the NIC gender-responsive project (Wright, Van Voorhis, Salisbur, & Bauman, 2012). One of their key findings is the need to pay particular attention to the hiring and training staff. Research has noted that, because females are more verbal and need to talk through their experiences of victimization and associated trauma, it is imperative that those working with women are more treatment-oriented and display positive interpersonal and communication skills (Koons-Witt, Burrow, Morash, & Bynum, 1997; Schram, Koons-Witt, & Morash, 2004; Wright et al., 2012). In addition, they also need adequate training which emphasizes an understanding of how victimization and trauma affect women in terms of their relationships, mental health, substance abuse, parenting practices, etc. (Hardyman & Van Voorhis, 2004; Wright et al., 2012).

The need for more specific training is equally as important when working with LGBTQ incarcerated girls and women, many of whom face additional or unique issues (Curtin, 2002; Majd, Marksamer, & Reyes, 2009). For example, Pasko's (2011) research highlights how young women regularly experience heteronormative policies and overall homophobia from both staff and other inmates. Not only do staff assume all young women are straight, policies are gender-conforming, and deviation from those expected norms often results in isolation and other punishment. Additionally, in Curtin's (2002) study, 'every participant reported witnessing openly homophobic peer behavior such as anti-gay name calling and threats of violence' (p.9). Pasko (2011) noted that while there is some recognition of the bias, harassment, and abuse of LGBTQ youth in custody, programming was non-existent despite the fact that there was a clear need for it. Wilber, Ryan, and Marksamer (2006) reported the findings and recommendations of *The Model Standards Project: Creating Inclusive Systems for LGBT Youth In Out-of-Home Care*. Their recommendations include: 1) creating an inclusive organizational culture; 2) recruiting and supporting competent staff; 3) promoting healthy adolescent development; 4) providing sensitive support services; and, 5) providing appropriate placements. Unfortunately, to date, these standards appear to be followed in words rather than action, and very little has changed.

Heterornormative Policies and Practices

The works of Wilber et al. (2006); Majd et al. (2009); Pasko (2011); Holsinger and Hodge (2016) all seek to identify heteronormative policies and procedures within the juvenile justice system that creates issues for LGBTQ youth. These studies identify numerous policies that discriminate against LGBTQ youth, including dressing in a feminine manner, hairstyle restrictions (including disallowing young women to shave their heads), offering heterosexual lifestyle and sex education, as well as reparative therapy.

The literature is replete with examples of how detention staff often hypersexualize LGBTQ youth and define benign interactions as sexual overtones towards others. Staff members often punish LGBTQ girls for behavior that was overlooked in heterosexual girls. For example, when girls were interacting with other girls and having fun, they were often accused of flirting, other behavior, such as hugging was deemed predatory and encouraging sexual behavior. This appeared to be especially so for Black girls. Irvine-Baker, Jones, and Canfield (2019) found that even non-romantic behavior such as braiding or styling one another's hair was viewed through a hypersexual lens. The young women felt that their behavior was overly scrutinized and feel as though they are being constantly harassed due to their sexual orientation.

Holsinger and Hodge (2016) found that the LGBTQ youth in their study were troubled by the double standards that exist. They felt that they were unfairly 'picked on' in a number of ways. They described situations where heterosexual girls could sit close together or hold hands without repercussions, yet they were punished (lost levels) for the exact same behavior (p.33). Furthermore, they complained that heterosexual girls were allowed to discuss their relationships in group, but LGBTQ girls could not. When the young women raised the issue of the double standard, their concerns were dismissed. Furthermore, Holsinger and Hodge (2016) noted that their interviews with staff confirmed the girls assessment that staff tended to view LGBTQ girls as both predatory and bullies (p.36). Thus, while there appear to be clear policies regarding behavior, the policies appear to be applied in a discriminatory manner.

The extent of abuse and discrimination of LGBTQ youth by their peers and staff is well documented, as has the extent that isolation and segregation to handle the problem. In their attempt to keep LGBTQ youth 'safe,' youth are often placed in segregation, rather than punishing the abusers (Beck, Harrison, & Guerino, 2010; Curtin, 2002; Hunt & Moodie-Mills, 2012; Irvine-Baker et al., 2019; Pasko, 2011). Estrada and Marksamer (2006) document the negative psychological impact that segregation and isolation have on youth. In 2012, mandates were added to the 2003 Prison Rape Elimination Act (PREA) to address this problem. These mandates require a change to this practice as well as more training of staff. As Owen, Wells, and Pollack (2017) noted, while the standards exist they have yet to be put into operational practices.

The Equity Project has identified a number of existent policy statements developed to address these issues. While they clearly state that harassment and discrimination are not acceptable, that staff should not make youth feel that they are abnormal, that the use of appropriate language and pronund use is imperative, and that staff shall not hold LGBTQ youth to different standards, discrimination and harassment persists. Thus, the required development of policies appears to be in name only. Research that raises this concern with staff report that their only suggestion for solving this issue is further training (Dean,

Victor, & Guidry-Grimes, 2016; Holsinger & Hodge, 2016; Irvine-Baker et al., 2019; Mitton-Kukner, Kearns, & Tompkins, 2016). There is clear evidence that the field of criminal justice has been slow to make the necessary adjustments in addressing the needs of incarcerated LGBTQ youth (especially girls and women), yet other disciplines such as health care, social work, and education have made great advancements in this area. Keeping in mind the underlying principles of GRP, our goal here is to use major interdisciplinary examples to expand two of the GRP principles in hopes of showing how correctional and organizational staff can be trained in becoming more 'queer-responsive' to the needs of LGBTQ girls and women.

Making GRP More Queer Responsive

There are several common components of gender-based programming: relationships, physical and emotional safety, attention to health, cultural appropriateness and competence, responses to sexism, strengths-based approaches, holistic approaches, family involvement, life skills, educational and vocational opportunities, and community opportunities (Treskon & Bright, 2017). If we expanded these components often associated with gender-responsive programming in relation to sexual orientation and non-gender binary identity, it would look like the following (new additions in italics):

> **Principles focus on relationships.** Relationships are used as the basis for personal change. Because of the relational nature of female development, *and the development of sexual orientation*, attention is paid to relationships between staff members and clients, and between clients and important people in their lives. *The importance of this takes on an amplified role when research shows that a disproportionate amount of abuse occurs to LGBTQ folks at the hands of those maintaining these specific positions of power.*
>
> **Safety**. Physical and emotional safety is essential, given the high rates of trauma and maltreatment in the populations served. Clients must be able to express themselves without fear of harm or reprisal. *We should ask ourselves, how LGBTQ folks are supposed to be able to do this when they are consistently rendered invisible by the system, and those working in it. Physical and emotional safety begins with acknowledgement and centering (not marginalizing) of ones identity. Furthermore, as noted* by Irvine, Wilber, and Canfield (2017), *classification and housing decisions should not be based on LGBTQ status and youth should not be isolated for protection purposes, nor should any youth be punished for departing from gender norms.*
>
> **Attention to health, mental health, and substance use**. Healthy living is a focus, and attention is paid to physical, behavioral, and reproductive health issues of relevance to women *and those within the LGBTQ community. LGBTQ folks have disproportionate health risks, mental health risks, and substance abuse issues. Thus, attention should be paid to the reasons for these risk factors within the context of LGBTQ lives. Programs must not only be culturally affirming, but should be cared for by medical staff that must adhere to relevant medical standards, and receive transition related health care. Furthermore, youth should never be subjected to any conversion therapies (*Irvine, Wilber, and Canfield, 2017).
>
> **Cultural appropriateness and competence**. Services are consistent with clients' cultural values. Racism and discrimination in the broader society are recognized, and services are designed to promote equality. Given that women of color, *poor people, and those who identify as LGBTQ,* are overrepresented in criminal and juvenile justice systems, cultural competence, or the ability to interact with people of different cultures, and an intersectional approach, in

which each person is understood as having a complex social identity, are particularly relevant. *In order to best respond to the needs of LGBTQ youth, programs must be culturally affirming*

Response to sexism *and Homophobia*. Female development is central to service provision, with a focus on the broader social forces that perpetuate sexism, *and heterosexism* in gender-based discrimination. *Required ongoing training of staff to educate them regarding how to work with LGBTQ youth, how to recognize, respond to and prevent harassment, how to assess the needs of LGBTQ youth, and how to create a professional environment, which is not heteronormative and accepting of differences. In addition, staff should use preferred names and pronouns of the youth.*

Strengths-based approach. Rather than concentrating on deficits, staff members actively identify and build on clients' individual strengths to promote their empowerment.

Holistic approach. Services focus on the well being of the whole person rather than treatment of a particular symptom or problem, in recognition of the complexities of girls' *and LGBTQ individual's* development. *For LGBTQ youth, this must also include support needs associated with coming out and bullying.*

Family involvement. Resolution of family conflict, common in girls' histories, and the development of positive family connections are a critical component of services. Family members are included in decisions and treatment. Individual and group activities focus on acknowledging and responding to interpersonal trauma and maltreatment, more commonly experienced by females than males. *In addition to gender, the focus on LGBTQ identities could not possibly be more crucial considering that a majority of trauma, and consequences of such, in LGBTQ lives comes from the family unit.*

Life skills. Clients develop skills needed to make the transition to adulthood. This may reduce reliance on unhealthy relationships and promote women's independence. *Dependency has been directly linked to IPV in LGBTQ relationships, thus, promoting this specific set of skills in LGBTQ lives, should also be considered. Additionally, when there is such a high proportion of homeless LGBTQ youth, we should also consider focusing on these skill sets that they may have never had the chance to develop in the first place.*

Educational and vocational opportunities. Clients learn about and have access to educational and job-related opportunities that prepare them to pursue any field of interest, not just female dominated professions. *In addition to instilling these same opportunities in LGBTQ folks, there is also an additional need to work with these folks on individualized occupational plans in which they learn how to navigate institutionalized homophobia in addition to sexism.*

Community opportunities. Connections to the wider community are encouraged through introductions and opportunities to join organizations or volunteer. *It is important to develop ties and partner with LGBTQ centers and advocates. It is necessary for staff to familiarize themselves with local programs that serve LGBTQ youth and make referrals upon the youths' release.* (Authors, 2019)

Just as gender-responsive programs cater to the unique pathways, issues, and needs of girls and young women, they must also be equipped to care for the pathways, issues, and needs of LGBTQ youth, especially LGBTQ girls and women (authors, 2019).

When building programs, there is great value in including the voices and experiences of those in custody, because it can be used both, as a learning tool and guideline for future programming. For example, Ginsburg et al. (2002) found that talking to LGBTQ youth about their needs was especially useful. Lesbian, gay, bisexual, transgender, and questioning youth in their study expressed the need for assurances of confidentiality, as well as clinicians who are nonjudgmental, honest, do not talk down to them, show respect and sensitivity, and are open-minded and educated with regard to LGBTQ issues. Additionally, they also indicated that when assumptions about heterosexuality and/or negative reactions to their sexual orientation were made, there could be no relationship with that professional. As a result, they suggested making a symbolic effort, which included the availability of LGBTQ-oriented magazines and books that gave them a sense that they were in a gay-friendly space. As mentioned earlier, Berberet (2006) found that LGBTQ youth in her study were concerned with a variety of safety measures, including protection from harassment, verbal, and physical aggression, and to not be treated differently due to sexual orientation or gender identity. Emerging staff in trainings that focus on certain elements of GRP will ensure that needs such as these are met.

While not all justice facilities and staff can be considered neglectful and/or overtly discriminatory (and even abusive) towards LGBTQ folks, there is an overwhelming amount of evidence that these issues persist. There is a clear need for better staff training that fully attempts to overcome these issues. As a result, we recommend formulating training that expands staff training on developing *cultural appropriateness*, and *competence* and *responses to sexism and homophobia*.

Cultural Appropriateness and Competence

Cultural competence refers to the set of attitudes, behaviors and policies to work effectively in cross-cultural setting. One of the most obvious measures of cultural competence is ones' language. The language a person uses demonstrates a person's attitudes, experiences, and knowledge. Thus, a staff member's use of language tells a patient, student, or client how open they are to understanding their lived experience and sets the tone for further interactions. As a starting point, staff must be aware of definitions and language and changes in such as they occur (Rossi & Lopez, 2017).

One of the basic tenets of gender-responsive programming is to provide an environment in which youth are safe and perceive themselves to be safe. But, what does it mean for an LGBTQ youth to believe that they are safe? Berberet (2006) assessed social service agencies which served LGBTQ youth in San Diego. Utilizing both questionnaires and focus groups with both staff and youth, she found that while the issue of safety was ranked as one of the youths' primary concerns, it was only mentioned (and often in an off-hand manner) by 20% of staff. When Berberet (2006) delved further, she found that there was a great disparity between the youth and staff definition of safety. When staff referred to safety as a concern, they were referring to the space outside (bad neighborhoods, violence perpetuated by strangers, etc.); however, the youth's concern was within the agency. LGBTQ youth's concern with safety referred to three concerns: 1) protection from verbal and physical aggression; 2) protection from harassment; 3) not treated differently due to sexual orientation or identity (p.381). Clearly, for programs to be effective with LGBTQ youth, there needs to be culturally appropriate and competent language use during interactions, which includes making sure that there is an agreed-upon definition of words and respect for pronouns.

In addition to building and understanding appropriate language and pronoun usage, another crucial component to the *cultural appropriateness and competence* element of GRP is the recognition of 'complex social identity,' and the importance of focusing on intersectionality. Research by Irvine, Canfield, and Roa (2017) accentuates this point by highlighting that services must take into account how race, sexual orientation, gender identity, and gender expression (SOGIE) directly pave girls' pathways into the justice system. The authors used three case studies to exemplify their points. In Diana's case, her gender expression and ethnicity would continue to be viewed as a threat to public safety regardless of her lack of gang affiliation. Erica must endure programs that exemplify heterosexual relationships (a framework that doesn't even apply to her) because she refuses to come out to her family and those working with her. Finally, Bebe is a black transwoman and has a difficult time finding counselors who serve transgender youth, as well as negative interactions with white, male police officers because of her identity. Each of these cases are examples of how an understanding of intersectionality is a must for all staff and service providers. Irvine, Canfield, and Roa go on to call out that system-involved LGBQ and GNCT girls 'will continue to remain marginalized as long as adults who are serving them continue to assume that only white youth are gay, to link gender non-conformity with gang affiliation and hyperaggressivity, and to view youth of color as hypersexual and predatory' (p. 217).

While county and state juvenile facilities have policies that state that juveniles in their care shall receive fair and equal treatment and shall not face discrimination or harassment by staff or other youth, often staff are unaware of what falls within these categories. Because of the lack of adequate training, they are unfamiliar with appropriate language, behavior, and overall understanding of the hardships of (intersecting) marginalized identity. There are a number of organizations that have developed programs that address this problem. These programs include the learning of shared definitions, examine the concept of SOGIE, and deconstruct myths and stereotypes (see for example the Equity Project, Lesson 1, OHYAC Training material, Rossi & Lopez, 2017).

Responding to Sexism and Homophobia

Those working with LGBTQ youth and adults, whether in social work, the medical field, schools, the justice system, and other systems of care, must examine their personal attitudes reflecting on homophobia and heteronormativity. It is necessary that staff acknowledge and understand their own personal biases and how they affect their interactions with others. This is especially true when those individuals are responsible for the care and custody of others. First, and foremost, it is imperative that staff do not make assumptions about a young women's' sexual orientation and gender identity. Staff must be adequately trained so that they are able to make individual assessments and not rely upon gender, race or other stereotypes. Toner's (2013) study of rural social workers found that staff acknowledged major gaps into their knowledge and recognized that within the discipline, there was a 'great deal of ignorance and prejudice regarding LGBTQ orientation and expression' (p.77). The findings suggest that a necessary first step in the educational process is to focus on staff's self-assessment and self-understanding of their attitudes toward sexual orientation, gender identity, and expression. In addition, they cite the need to direct agencies to the multitude of research and training materials (Elze & McHalen, 2009; Fostering Transitions, 2012; National Center for Lesbian Rights, 2006; Out of Home Youth Advocacy Council, 2007).

Research regarding the disparities in health care recognized that despite the fact that LGBTQ patients want the same basic, high-quality care, they do not always receive it. For example, research indicates that a large number of health-care providers acknowledge that they had never received training and, as a result, were uncomfortable discussing these issues. Whatever training they had received, came about as part of broad diversity training at conferences. Thus, recent literature directs medical schools to incorporate training to deal with sexual minority patients throughout their medical school training (Gahagan & Subirana-Malaret, 2018). In order to address this issue, the health professional literature is replete with tools for training medical professionals. As outlined by Harrison (1996), medical staff are to have non-homophobic attitudes, be able to distinguish between sexual identity and behavior, communicate using proper terminology and pronouns, and be aware of how their own attitudes can affect clinical judgment.

A key to maintaining a comprehensive gender-responsive program is to create a safe space for young women (heterosexual and non-heterosexual; cisgender and gender variant) to heal. Not only does this entail a nurturing, safe environment, but a safe, non-discriminatory physical space. Pennell (2017) describes an exercise that she uses with teachers and school administrators in the educational setting that would also be useful to tool to utilize with correctional staff to assess the physical environment. After explaining and discussing heteronormativity, she has the participants go on a heteronormativity 'Scavenger Hunt' in order to 'explore the physical space to look for examples and counter-examples of heteronormativity ... Participants then look for signs of LGBTQ inclusion, and those that are queer-friendly. Participants then discuss what they found, making lists of heteronormativity and queer-affirming examples' (p.65). She finds that participants are generally surprised to find the extent of heteronormativity ingrained in our physical spaces. Upon completion of this exercise, she asks the participants to brainstorm together and then develop an action plan to create a more 'queer-friendly' space (Pennell, 2017). Exercises such as these are necessary to allow staff to gain perspective before they begin assessing their policies and procedures to make them more queer-responsive.

Criminal justice programs should be encouraged to include issues specific to LGBTQ offenders throughout the curriculum. This should be accomplished by the inclusion of LGBTQ issues as part of the diversity strand, often found in a variety of existing classes and by creating classes that address LGBTQ-specific issues that are relevant at each stage of the criminal justice system. However, rather than simply focusing on individual issues, such as bullying, suicide and discrimination, classes need to examine structural oppression, so that students may understand the underlying problems that create homophobic and transphobic environments (Goldstein, Russell, & Daley, 2007; Loutzenhouser & MacIntosh, 2004; MacIntosh, 2007). Training for in-service staff must be mandatory, ongoing, and tailored to the specific professional responsibilities of the audience (i.e. judges, defense attorneys, prosecutors, probation officers and detention staff). Agencies should also form committees to continually review and propose policies to ensure that institutional change does occur within their respective organizations. In addition, Dean et al. (2016), also encourage administrators and staff to read literature and biographies written by LGBTQ authors, become familiar with Kevin Nadel's (2013)*That's so Gay: Microaggression and the Lesbian, Gay, Bisexual and Transgender Community*, and take part in LGBTQ community events. Other meams of training should also be utilized in addition to in-service trainings on diversity issues.

Group work

Dean et al. (2016) offer insight as to why diversity training on LGBTQ issues is good, but not the only type of training that should occur. As they note, diversity training and changes to policy may reduce explicit forms of discrimination, but they may not reduce implicit, or less overt forms of discrimination. They attribute this to microaggressions – brief, nuanced and often unintentional slights and offenses that underlie verbal and nonverbal communication (Sue, 2010). They contend that, while the individual training mentioned above is necessary, there is a need to include groupwork that addresses the schemas underlying heteronormative microaggressions and how they are socially produced. This is important since it is often easier for individuals to acknowledge these behaviors at a societal level and are less likely to become defensive. Training must be ongoing, and following training supervisors must hold individuals responsible for microaggressions as they occur and remind them of the harm caused. In other words, continuous training, coaching and modeling must be available.

Similarly, Luke and Goodrich (2013) describe and assess an LGBTQ Responsive Model utilizing group work with school counselors. They, too, believe that in order to make school culture less heterosexist and eliminate harassment of LGBTQ students, training must go beyond the existent diversity training. They advocate for a supervisory model based on Bernard's (1979) Discrimination Model, in which the groups focus can be on: (1) conceptualization (how a supervisor, teacher, counselor thinks about their client); (2) personalization (the reactions, biases, or history that may influence their work with a client; and (3) intervention (the techniques or skills used or not used with clients) (Luke & Goodrich, p, 125).

The overall purpose is to understand how one's culture, history and bias influence their interaction and development of skills. They assert that ongoing training, and the utilization of real-world examples is necessary for skill development. They also suggest that staff (in this case teachers and counselors) keep a weekly reflective journal where they document their interactions with LGBTQ youth and note what skills they learned and utilized, how they felt (what was comfortable and uncomfortable), and what they wished they knew. These journal entries were then used to create further group trainings.

In sum, there are a variety of reasons for needing gender-responsive programs to also be queer-responsive. While all principles of GRP are important, using the principles of *cultural appropriateness* and *competence*, and *responses to sexism and homophobia* as means to guide staff trainings would significantly improve the lives and experiences of system-involved LGBTQ girls and women. There is no doubt that safer enviroments will emerge as staff begin to develop an understanding of language, and recognize how each person brings with them a unique positionality – one that contains their own set of intersecting hardships – which may require a different set of services and responses. In addition, training staff to respond to sexism and homophobia by addressing personal bias, incorporating a variety training methods for understanding LGBTQ issues and microaggressions, encouraging staff to read LGBTQ literature, and encouraging staff to play an active role in LGBTQ community events will only improve the relationships between staff and those they are supervising. Based on all the interdisciplinary examples put forth here, recommendations that have formerly failed to take root in facilities will certainly thrive.

Conclusion

Criminal justice programming and facilities are not built to accommodate the needs of LGBTQ youth and adults. Research shows that LGBTQ girls and women have unique pathways into the system that include disproportionate rates of: victimization, homelessness, family conflict, child welfare involvement, and even sentencing disparities (Dank et al., 2014; Freedner et al., 2002; Hunt & Moodie-Mills, 2012; Kann et al., 2014; Valentino, 2011). Once in the system, LGBTQ youth (especially girls and women) have been rendered invisible (Irvine, 2010), experienced prejudice, ignorance, double standards, and hypersexualization at the hands of staff (Holsinger & Hodge, 2016; Irvine-Baker et al., 2019; Toner, 2013), reported serious issues with safety, and isolation as a result of safety issues (Berberet, 2006; Curtin, 2002; Hunt & Moodie-Mills, 2012), and been subject to numerous heteronormative policies and procedures (Majd et al., 2009; Pasko, 2011; Wilber et al., 2006). It is our intention here to show that much of this can be avoided by training criminal justice administration and staff in these specific areas.

In order to improve the wellbeing and overall healing of system-involved LGBTQ girls and women, we move forward in recommending a significant part of a solution by focusing, in depth, on how staff can be trained in *cultural appropriateness and competence* and *responses to sexism and homophobia*. All things considered, our work here aligns with the recommendations put forth by several authors. These recommendations include: 1) creating and upholding policies that protect LGBTQ individuals, 2) prioritizing staff training on LGBTQ issues, 3) fostering institutionalized respect for LGBTQ folks by creating inclusive cultures, and 4) specifically collecting data on sexual orientation, gender identity, and expression of system-involved LGBTQ individuals (see Garnette, Irvine, Reyes, & Wilber, 2011; Irvine et al., 2017; Wakefield & Spivak, 2016).

In conclusion, it is important to think about how LGBTQ youth, especially girls and women, can be better supported within the constraints of the criminal and juvenile justice systems. As outlined in Irvine-Baker et al. (2019, p. 333), 'If the juvenile justice system must exist, it should be a system that is sensitive and responsive to the developmental needs of youth and organized around principles and practices that are known to encourage healthy adolescent development.' In thinking about this, we, as a society, must include ALL youth, especially those occupying non-heterosexual and non-gender binary identities.

Disclosure statement

No potential conflict of interest was reported by the authors.

References

Adopting a trauma-informed approach for LGBTQ youth: A two-part resource for schools and agencies. (n.d.). Retrieved from https://healthysafechildren.org/sites/default/files/Trauma_Informed_Approach_LGBTQ_Youth_1.pdf

Beck, A., Harrison, P., & Guerino, P. (2010). *Sexual victimization in juvenile facilities reported by youth.* Washington, D.C.: U.S. Department of Justice, Bureau of Justice Statistics.

Belknap, J., Holsinger, K., & Little, J. (2014). Lesbian, Gay, and Bisexual youth incarcerating in delinquent facilities. In D. Peterson & V. Panfil (Eds.), *Handbook of LGBT communities, crime, and justice* (pp. 207–228). New York: Springer.

Berberet, H. (2006). Putting the pieces together for queer youth: A model of integrated assessment of need and program planning. *Child Welfare, 85*(2), 361–384.

Bernard, J.M. (1979). Supervisor training: A discrimination model. *Counselor Education & Supervision, 19*(1), 60–68.

Bloom, B., Owen, B., & Covington, S. (2003). *Gender-responsive strategies: Research, practice, and guiding principles for women offenders.* Washington, D.C.: Department of Justice: National Institute of Corrections.

Covington, S., & Bloom, B. (2000). *Gendered justice: Programming for women in correctional settings.* Paper presented at the 52nd Annual Meeting of the *American Society of Criminology*, San Francisco, California.

Curtin, M. (2002). Lesbian and bisexual girls in the juvenile justice system. *Child and Adolescent Social Work Journal, 19*(4), 285–301.

Dank, M., Lachman, P., Zweig, J., & Yahner, J. (2014). Dating violence experiences of lesbian, gay, bisexual, and transgender youth. *Journal of Youth and Adolescence, 43*(5), 846–857.

Dean, M.A., Victor, E., & Guidry-Grimes, L. (2016). Inhospitable healthcare spaces: Why diversity training on LGBTQIA issues is not enough. *Journal of Bioethical Inquiry, 13*(4), 557–570.

Elze, D., & McHalen, R. (2009). *Moving the margins: Training curriculum for child welfare services with lesbian, gay, bisexual, transgender and questioning youth in out-of-home care.* New York: Lambda Legal.

Estrada, R., & Marksamer, J. (2006). Lesbian, gay, bisexual and transgender young people in state custody: Making the child welfare and juvenile justice systems safe for all youth through litigation, advocacy and education. *Temple Law Review, 79*(2), 1–19.

Feinstein, R., Greenblatt, A., Hass, L., Kohn, S., & Rana, J. (2001). *Justice for all? A report on Lesbian, Gay, Bisexual, and Transgender Youth in the New York Juvenile Justice System.* (Information Analyses). Urban Justice Center.

Fostering Transitions: A CWLA/Lambda Legal Joint Initiative (2012). *Getting down to basics: Tools to support LGBTQ youth in care*. Retrieved from http://www.lambdalegal.org/sites/default/files/gdtb_2013_cmplete.pdf.

Freedner, N., Freed, L., Yang, W., & Austin, B. (2002). Dating violence among Gay, lesbian, and bisexual adolescents: Results from a community survey. *Journal of Adolescent Health*, *31*(6), 469–474.

Gahagan, J., & Subirana-Malaret, M. (2018). Improving pathways to primary health care among LGBTQ populations and health care providers: Key findings from Nova Scotia, Canada. *International Journal of Equity Health*, *17*(1), 76.

Garnette, L., Irvine, A., Reyes, C., & Wilber, S. (2011). Lesbian, Gay, Bisexual, and Transgender (LGBT) youth and the juvenile justice system. In F. Sherman & F. Jacobs (Eds.), *promoting health and well being in the juvenile justice system* (pp. 156–173). New Jersey: John Wiley & Sons.

Ginsburg, K.R., Winn, R.J., Rudy, B.J., Crawford, J., Zhao, H., & Schwarz, D.F. (2002). How to reach sexual minority youth in the health care setting: The teens offer guidance. *Journal of Adolescent Health*, *31*(5), 407–416.

Goldstein, T., Russell, V., & Daley, A. (2007). Safe, positive and queering moments in teaching education and schooling: A conceptual framework. *Teaching Education*, *18*(3), 183–199.

Hardyman, P.L., & Van Voorhis, P. (2004). *Developing gender-specific classification systems for women offenders*. Washington, DC: U.S. Department of Justice, National Institute of Corrections.

Harrison, A.E. (1996). Primary care of lesbian and gay patients: Educating ourselves and our students. *Family Medicine*, *28*(1), 10–23.

Herek, G.M. (1990). The context of anti-gay violence notes on cultural and psychological heterosexism. *Journal of Interpersonal Violence*, *5*(3), 316–333.

Himmelstein, K.E.W., & Bruckner, H. (2011). Criminal justice and school sanctions against nonheterosexual youth: A national longitudinal study. *Journal of Pediatrics*, *127*(1), 48–56.

Holsinger, K., & Hodge, J. (2016). The experiences of lesbian, gay, bisexual and transgender girls in juvenile justice systems. *Feminist Criminology*, *11*(1), 23–47.

Hunt, J., & Moodie-Mills, A. (2012). *The unfair criminalization of gay and transgender youth: An overview of the experiences of LGBT youth in juvenile justice*. Washington, DC: Center for American Progress.

Irvine, A. (2010). "We've had three of them:" Addressing the invisibility of lesbian, gay, bisexual, and gender non-conforming youths in the juvenile justice system. *Columbia Journal of Gender and Law*, *19*(3), 675–701.

Irvine, A. (2016). The overrepresentation of lesbian, gay, bisexual, questions, gender nonconforming and transgender youth within the child welfare to juvenile justice crossover population. *Journal of Gender, Social Policy, & the Law*, *24*(2), 243–261.

Irvine, A., Canfield, A., & Roa, J. (2017). Lesbian, bisexual, questions, gender-nonconforming, and transgender (LGBQ/GNCT) girls in the juvenile justice system: Using an intersectional lens to develop gender-responsive programming. In C. Datchi & J. Ancis (Eds.), *Gender, psychology, and justice: The mental health of women and girls in the legal system* (pp. 200–223). New York: New York University Press.

Irvine, A., & Canfield, A. (2017). Reflections on new national data on LGBQ/GNCT youth in the justice system. *LGBTQ Policy Journal at the Harvard Kennedy School*, *VII*, 27–36.

Irvine, A., Wilber, S., & Canfield, A. (2017). *Lesbian, Gay, Bisexual, Questioning, and gender nonconforming girls and boys in the California juvenile justice system: A practice guide*. Oakland, CA: Impact Justice and the National Center for Lesbian Rights.

Irvine-Baker, A., Jones, N., & Canfield, A. (2019). Taking the "girl" out of gender-responsive programming in the juvenile justice system. *Annual Review of Criminology*, *2*(1), 321–336.

Kahle, L., & Rosenbaum, J. (2019). Making gender responsive programming more queer responsive. In H. Pontell (Ed.), *Oxford research encyclopedia of criminology and criminal justice*.

Kann, L., Kinchen, S., Shanklin, S., Flint, K., Hawkins, J., Harris, W., Lowry, R., O'Malley, E., McManus, T., Chyen, D., Whittle, L., Taylor, E., Demissie, Z., Brener, N., Thornton, J., Moore, J., & Zaza, S. (2014). *Youth risk behavior surveillance-United States, 2013* (Surveillance Summary No. 4). Center for Disease Control and Prevention.

Koons-Witt, B.A., Burrow, J.D., Morash, M., & Bynum, T. (1997). Expert and offender perceptions of program elements linked to successful outcomes for incarcerated women. *Crime and Delinquency*, *43*, 513–532.

Loutzenhouser, L., & MacIntosh, L. (2004). Citizenships, sexualities and education. *Theory and Practice.*, *43*(2), 151–158.

Luke, M., & Goodrich, K. (2013). Investigating the LGBTQ responsive model for supervision of group work.". *The Journal for Specialists in Group Work*, *38*(2), 121–145.

MacIntosh, L. (2007). Does anyone have a band aid? Anti-homophobia discourses and pedagogical impossibilities. *Educational Studies*, *41*(1), 33–43.

Majd, K., Marksamer, J., & Reyes, C. (2009). *Hidden injustice: Lesbian, gay, bisexual and transgender youth in juvenile courts*. Legal Services for Children, National Juvenile Defender Center and National Center for Lesbian Rights. http://www.nclrights.org/wp-content/uploads/2014/06/hidden_injustice.pdf

Marksamer, J., & Tobin, L.H. (2014). *Standing with LGBT prisoners: An advocate's guide to ending abuse and combating imprisonment*. Washington, DC: National Center for Transgender Equality.

Messinger, A. (2017). *LGBTQ intimate partner violence*. Oakland, CA: University of California Press.

Mitton-Kukner, J., Kearns, L.L., & Tompkins, J. (2016). Pre-service educators and anti-oppressive pedagogy: Interrupting and challenging LGBTQ oppression in schools. *Asia-Pacific Journal of Teacher Education*, *44*(1), 20–34.

Nadal, K. L. (2013). *That's so gay!: Microaggressions and the Lesbian, Gay, Bisexual, and Transgender community*. American Psychological Association. doi:10.1037/14093-000.

National Center for Lesbian Rights. (2006). *Breaking the silence: Lesbian, gay, transgender, and queer foster youth tell their stories: A tool for working effectively with LGBTQ youth. DVD set*. San Francisco. Retrieved from http://www.nclrights.org.site/Docserver/NCLR_DVDorderform.pdf

Out of Home Youth Advisory Council (2007). *Creating inclusive services for LGBTQ youth in out of home care*. San Francisco: National Center for Lesbian Rights. Retrieved from http://www.nclrights.org/siite/DocServer/Preface_OHYAC_training_Final.pdf

Owen, B., Wells, J., & Pollack, J. (2017). *In search of safety*. Berkeley: University of California Press.

Pasko, L. (2011). Setting the record straight: Girls, sexuality, and juvenile correctional system. *Social Justice*, *37*(1), 7–24.

Pennell, S. (2017). Training secondary teachers to support LGBTQ+ students: Practical applications from theory and research. *The High School Journal*, *101*(1), 63–72.

Quinn, M., Poirier, J., & Garfinkel, L. (2005). Girls with mental health needs in the Juvenile Justice System: Challenges and inequities confronting a vulnerable population. *Exceptionality*, *13*(2), 125–139.

Renzetti, C.M. (1992). *Violent betrayal: Partner abuse in lesbian relationships*. United States: SAGE Publications.

Rossi, A., & Lopez, E. (2017). Contextualizing competence: Language and LGBT-based competency in health care.". *Journal of Homosexuality*, *64*(10), 1321–1364.

Schram, P.J., Koons-Witt, B.A., & Morash, M. (2004). Management strategies when working with female prisoners. *Women & Criminal Justice*, *15*(2), 25–50.

Sue, D. (2010). *Microaggressions and marginality: Manifestation, dynamics, and impact*. New York: Wiley.

Toner, J. (2013). Rural social workers' perception of training needs for working with LGBTQ identified youth in foster care. *Contemporary Rural Social Work Journal*, *5*(1), 65–84.

Treskon, L., & Bright, C. (2017). *Bringing gender-responsive principles into practice*. MDRI. https://www.mdrc.org/sites/default/files/PACE_brief_March2017_web.pdf

Valentino, A. (2011). LGBTQ youth in the juvenile justice system. *Children's Rights Litigation, American Bar Association*, *13*, 4.

Wakefield, C., & Spivak, A. (2016). Lesbian, gay, bisexual, transgender, and queer offenders: Sexual orientation, gender identity, and incarceration. In K. Dodson (Ed.), *Routledge handbook on special populations*

Wilber, S., Ryan, C., & Marksamer, J. (2006). *CWLA best practice guidelines*. Washington, DC: Child Welfare League of America. Retrieved from http://www.cyfdivision.com/documents/2778_Best_Practices_LGBTQ_5-06.pdf

Wright, E.M., Van Voorhis, P., Salisbur, E., & Bauman, A. (2012). Gender-responsive lessons learned and policy implications for women in prison: A review. *Criminal Justice and Behavior, 39*(12), 1612–1632.

Index

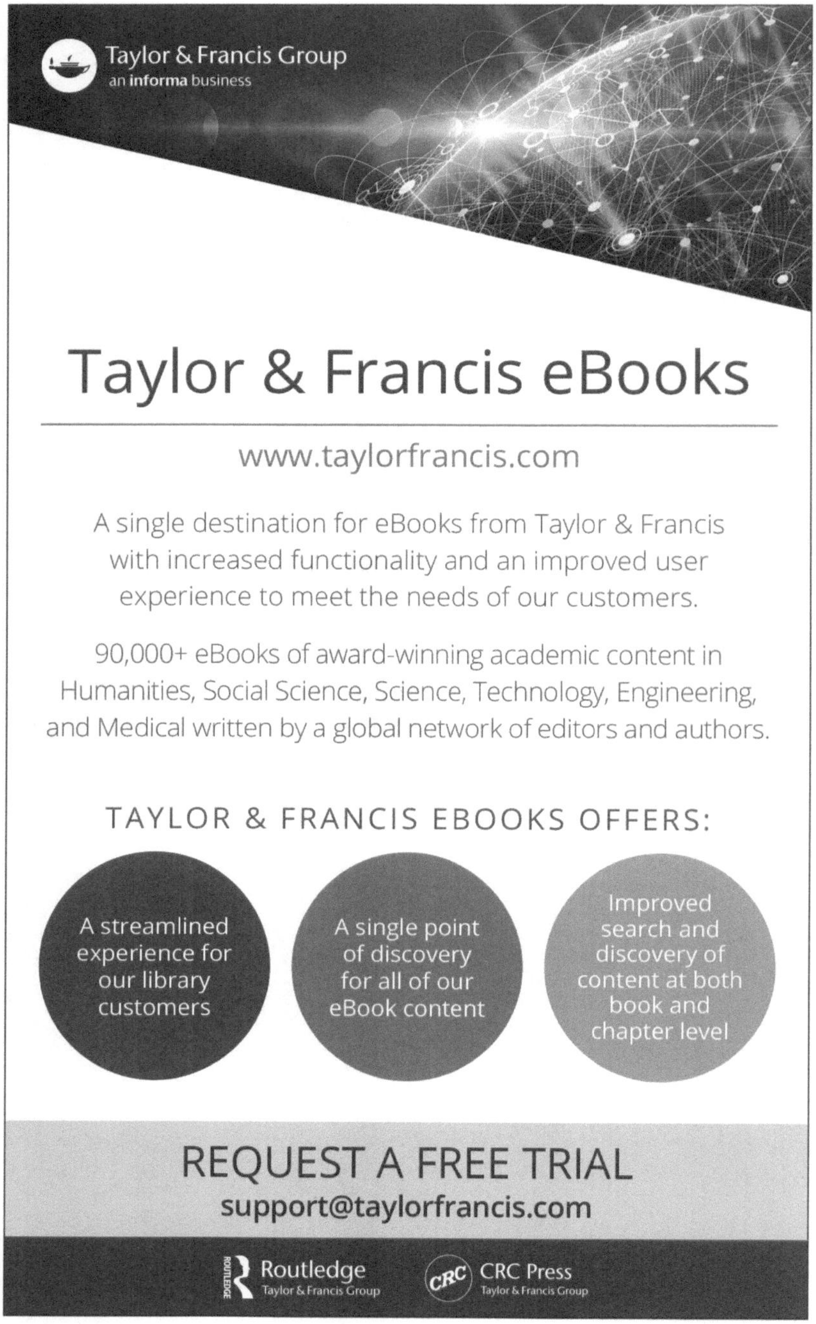